ADVENTURER EXTRAORDINARY

ADVENTURER EXTRAORDINARY

The Tiger Sarll Story

by

GODFREY LIAS

With a Foreword by
ÉAMONN ANDREWS

THE ADVENTURERS CLUB

LONDON

THE ADVENTURERS CLUB
178-202 Great Portland Street, London, W.1

First published by Cassell & Co. Ltd. 1961
This edition 1964

This book has been printed in Great Britain by litho-offset
by William Clowes and Sons Ltd, London and Beccles

FOREWORD

IF, quickly, I had to identify Tiger Sarll to viewers of the B.B.C.'s 'This is Your Life', I'd forget about the monocle and the six foot four erectness of the soldier and even the near incredible incidents from his story.

I'd simply say:

'Remember the man who, when we brought his grown family on one after another, stopped one of them and said, ''You're not one of mine, are you? Which one are you?'''

He probably infuriated every woman in the audience—and the happy, robust family reunion afterwards was too late to assuage the feelings of outraged parenthood.

But that's Tiger Sarll, the wanderer, the adventurer, the soldier of fortune, the Spartan who puts sentiment and affection way down the line and who's not prepared to murmur with the rest of us a hypocritical, 'How nice to meet you again.' More likely, 'And who the hell are you?'

Godfrey Lias has had the chance we didn't have of talking to the Tiger himself before telling his story. So I've no doubt at all that the pages that follow will tell us something much larger than life and much more exciting than any six of us could achieve.

This extraordinary adventurer frightens the wits out of me every time we meet. It's safer to read about him than to meet him.

ÉAMONN ANDREWS

CONTENTS

ILLUSTRATIONS

Between pages 94–95

Tiger's father—John Thomas Sarll, B.A.

Tiger, aged nine, with the snake which was a present from Mary Kingsley

A general view of Tangier in 1905
 (*Radio Times Hulton Picture Library*)

A typical street in Buenos Aires at the beginning of the century (*Radio Times Hulton Picture Library*)

A page of Captain Sarll's dispatches home from the front during the Balkan War in 1912 (*Central News*)

'A Show Worth Seeing': a poster for 'Rais' Sarll's circus

'Rais' Sarll with two of his snakes: a venomous horned snake and a nineteen-foot python

With two members of his circus: a newly arrived snake and a three-foot alligator
 (*Radio Times Hulton Picture Library*)

Captain and Mrs. Sarll at their home at Bradwell-on-Sea
 (*Maldon and Burnham Standard*)

Tiger as B.B.C. Television viewers saw him with Éamonn Andrews in the 'This is Your Life' programme
 (*British Broadcasting Association*)

ix

1. GROWING UP—TO SIX FEET FOUR INCHES

O NE of 'Tiger' Sarll's earliest memories is being hauled
ignominiously back from the window-ledge of his mother's
bedroom in Highgate when about to parachute to the garden
path below with the aid of his father's umbrella.

Tiger, who appears to have been about three, claims to remember the incident perfectly. He adds that he was simply
going to put into practice what he had seen grown-ups doing
from balloons over Alexandra Park. Being already nearly up
to the average grown-up's shoulder, he did not see why the
mere question of age should stop him from following his elders'
example.

So he was highly indignant when his father seized him by
the seat of the pants and hauled him back.

I am sure it was not Tiger's first escapade any more than it
was his last. All through his life, wherever trouble was to be
had for the travelling, Tiger did his best to get there. It is
true to say that facing death has been the very breath of his
life since the day he was born—23rd September 1882. That is
to say, for nearly four-score years.

His first rendezvous with death came actually before he was
born. He was one of twins and the first was dead when it
arrived—a whole month before Tiger himself came into the
world. His mother, and the doctor who attended her, both
told him in later years that he weighed sixteen and a half
pounds. His sister, Rosa, who is four years his senior, remembers only that he was at least three feet long. His mother, a
small, slight, beautiful woman measured exactly five feet. His
father was an inch taller and Rosa herself an inch above that.

Tiger, however, went on growing and had topped six feet
by the time he was twelve. He now stands six feet four inches
in his bare feet—bare because he no longer wears socks. He
explains that if he did, he would not be able to get his feet into
the largest size of ready-made shoes, and he does not see why
he should waste money on having shoes specially made for him.

He was not always of that opinion. There was a time when

he invariably wore a top-hat, morning coat, spats and patent leather boots. But he has been as lavish with his money as with his chances of survival. When he has made money, he has spent it. And then made some more. At the moment he is at the stage of having spent it.

Family tradition declares that when Rosa was introduced to her new brother, she said to her mother: 'Shall we drown it?' Her own version is that she suggested sitting on it. Even then, Tiger would have taken some sitting on and it has become progressively harder to do so ever since. The moment he scents any kind of danger, he crouches for the spring. Indeed, he justified his nickname long before he got it during the Boer War at the age of seventeen. His comrades in the South African Light Horse (Winston Churchill's regiment) noticed that when he was about to engage the enemy, he emitted something between a purr and a growl. So they called him Tiger. The name stuck.

Tiger's father, John Thomas Sarll, ran the University Institute, a well-known educational establishment near Regent's Park, London. The Sarlls moved from Mornington Road where Tiger was born to Highgate, Redhill and elsewhere before settling in Bloomsbury at number 64 Gower Street in about 1890. Their house was pulled down years ago and the Royal School of Dramatic Art now stands in its place.

For some reason or other, Tiger was not christened till he was twelve—possibly because his parents were waiting for water from the River Jordan to do it with. They not only gave him the names Thomas William Henry which he still uses (though only when absolutely necessary) but added Bang-fee which he has discarded. They told him that Bang-fee is Chinese for eagle, and among his archives is an elaborate Bang-fee written in Chinese characters given him by the Chinese Minister in London who was a frequent visitor at the Sarlls' house. He generally came with a tiny Pekinese in the ample sleeve of his mandarin's robe—perhaps the first of the breed that was ever seen in England.

The Sarlls' friendship with the Chinese Minister sprang from the fact that Tiger's mother, whose name before she married was Rosa Braden, came from a family with a long tradition as importers of tea from China. Tiger's maternal grandfather lived in Hankow for many years. Those were the days when the *Cutty Sark, Flying Cloud* and other famous tea clippers raced dangerously round half the world with far too many sails set in the hope of being first home with their precious cargoes.

They were also the days when the Chinese Government insisted on confining the despised western races to 'concessions' where they were governed by special laws called 'capitulations' because they were not fit to receive the protection of the laws which applied to the 'Celestials'. Braving the contempt of the 'Celestials' in those pioneering times required great courage. So did braving their cupidity when the concessions came to prosper beyond expectation. Tiger's sister, Rosa, was living there when the Chinese wrested the concessions back by force. She had become Mrs. Spenceley by this time.

The Chinese Minister was not the only member of the Legation who visited the Sarlls and, about a year after Bang-fee's christening, a junior Chinese official confided to them that a certain notorious Sun Yat-sen was being held prisoner in the Legation with a view to his being smuggled out of the country and taken back to China to have his head cut off after the usual unspeakable preliminaries.

Bang-fee Tiger had been bound to secrecy but not to inaction; so he betook himself forthwith to Portland Place to try to effect a rescue on his own. After careful thought, he decided that the most promising plan was to ring the bell and say he wanted to see one of his friends. Having thus got inside, he would slip away unobserved, make his way to the cellar in which he understood that the prisoner was confined, release him and then fight his way out with his fists.

Unfortunately, every friend he asked for 'happened' to be 'out'. So Tiger never got inside the door. He was half-relieved, half-disappointed when Sun Yat-sen himself managed to smuggle a message out and the British Government rescued him. But, if we take the will for the deed, Tiger was very close to playing a part in the birth of modern China. His sister, Rosa, certainly did a few years later, but this is not her story.

In the days of his extreme youth, Tiger was known as 'Willie'. Indeed his first sweetheart, whose name is now Mrs.

Georgina Jack, wrote to him as 'dearest Willie' when she heard of him after a lapse of some seventy-five years. She and Tiger went to the same kindergarten in Highgate and he was supposed to act as her escort. Why she should remember him with any affection at all is surprising, seeing the way he interpreted his mission.

Georgina used to wear a very short, flouncy skirt over very frilly white drawers. Tiger, who had already acquired a pea-shooter, used to pepper her, and especially the drawers, with balls of blotting-paper dipped in ink.

Tiger's youthful, and not so youthful, escapades have been legion but by no means all of them have been mischievous ones. On his way home from school one afternoon, without Georgina, Tiger saw two boys ill-treating a cat. He was four and they were both about seven but he sailed into the pair of them at once, determined to teach them that cruelty, at any rate, is one of the crimes that do not pay.

His nurse, who ought to have been at the kindergarten in time to take him home, arrived on the scene to find Tiger giving at least as good as he got from the other two.

After she had separated the combatants, she rebuked the cat-baiters.

'You ought to be ashamed of yourselves,' she told them, 'hitting a little boy of four.'

''E ain't fower,' the culprits objected. ''E's bigger'n us. Lots. An', anyway, 'e 'it us fust.'

'You shouldn't have been hurting that poor pussy,' Tiger shouted at them. 'If you do it again, I'll kill you. Both of you.'

He still would. At the age of seventy-seven, he snatched a rifle away from two young men who had been shooting at swans—ones which had grown tame after he had cleansed them of oil—and broke it in two across his knee. As local Secretary (unpaid) of the R.S.P.C.A. at Bradwell-on-Sea, Essex, his house, The Oasis, is a repository for sick animals and birds of all sorts and descriptions, especially cats of which he generally has about six, all saved from being, as the phrase is, put away. The first time I went to see him there were four curled up in the kitchen alongside a seagull with a damaged wing. The kitchen is close to the bathroom and when either Tiger, or his wife, had a bath, the seagull hopped in too.

In the yard were two vast and friendly Labradors, a tame rook and a crow. The two birds were wild ones which had elected to stay on after Tiger had attended to their wounds— both had been shot. The rook greeted me with a succession of bows which accompanied words I could not make out. Then he remarked 'Hullo, Tommy Sarll', which is the name of Tiger's youngest son.

The crow got no further than a word which sounded like 'beggar' though it was possibly another word which Tiger never uses. Whatever it was, the crow just picked it up without any actual teaching.

Tiger's love of animals is not confined to warm-blooded ones. One of his pets between the two world wars was an anaconda which was over twenty-nine feet long—possibly the largest ever brought to England. During the Boer War he fought for more than two hours to prevent two of his fellow soldiers from roasting a tortoise alive. He holds that it is only right to kill an animal to put it out of pain, or if it is dangerous.

Yet he has killed many men, as we shall see, though only in fair fight and when defending himself, or others.

One day when he and I were walking along the Charing Cross Road—he had taken me to call on Christina Foyle who is a very old friend—we happened to pass a woman selling copies of a pacifist journal.

Tiger stopped at once to give battle.

'Are you a meat-eater, madam?' he began, fixing her balefully with his eye-glass.

'Yes, why?' she replied.

'Then you don't mind poor, helpless animals being killed,' Tiger growled. 'Only human beings.'

'But that's different,' she protested.

'Different?' Tiger roared. 'Of course it's different. Do the animals attack you?'

'Well, no,' the woman admitted. 'But what has that got to do with war? I can see you have been a soldier. Don't you think it's dreadful, deliberately killing one's fellow men? Human beings. Like ourselves.'

5

'As a soldier, madam,' Tiger told her, 'I killed in self-defence and in defence of my country. Or to punish evildoers. You kill, or cause other people to do so, merely to satisfy your appetite. You are a hypocrite, madam.'

Then he raised his beret politely (though with indifferent success—berets are non-cooperative) and stalked off.

Tiger was seven, or perhaps eight, when Mrs. Annie Besant said to him:

'Never eat meat. Never cut down a tree for it has life. Never kill, except in self-defence. Never pray to God *for* anything, but only to thank Him.'

Tiger thinks it would be going too far never to cut down a tree. Indeed, he aided and abetted tree-fellers when he drove teams for them in Canada fifty-seven years ago. But he has used Mrs. Besant's form of prayer regularly ever since and he has been a vegetarian in spite of strong pressure from his parents who kept on telling him (Heaven knows why!) that he would waste away if he did not eat meat. At seven he was already taller than either of them and he went on growing just as fast as before until he was fourteen. Since then, he has simply added a certain amount of muscle and an inch or two to his circumference.

Today, seventy years after his first meeting with Mrs. Besant, he thinks of her as a tall, imposing figure wearing a frilly lace cap which he had no impish desire to besmirch with his pea-shooter.

When Tiger's parents settled in Gower Street, Bloomsbury was still in its heyday. The Sarlls' neighbours were mostly well-to-do professional people—doctors, dentists, lawyers, politicians—in fact, Forsytes generally. Gower Street was almost as cluttered up with their horse carriages as it is today with horseless ones. And there was a constant jingle of hansom cabs as well as the rumble of four-wheelers. This was partly because the surface was better than in the nearby Tottenham Court Road but also because Gower Street boasted a cabby's shelter which provided food for its patrons.

The food did not attract Tiger—it was mostly meat. But the horses did. Their drivers had a way of leaving them outside unattended while they themselves gorged inside and the horses, becoming impatient, often decided to find their own way home. They reckoned, however, without Tiger. Whenever he could make the opportunity, from the age of eight onwards, he kept an eagle eye on such runaways, racing after them, clambering precariously into the cabby's seat and driving them back to the shelter.

According to Rosa, he also stopped a number of carriages whose horses had actually run away with passengers in them. She remembers him coming home one afternoon when he was about ten or eleven with blood streaming down his leg. He refused to have the wound attended to, saying it was nothing. Nor would he tell anyone how he got it and his family did not find out till one of the servants heard about it from an errand-boy. The boy said there were four people in a dog-cart when the horse got out of control. Tiger had run after it, jumped in at the back and taken the reins from the terrified driver.

The Sarlls were well off, and one of those who enjoyed their hospitality was Campbell Bannerman, the future Prime Minister. Another was Lord Randolph Churchill who was already the father of Winston. Others included Sir Edmund Gosse, the librarian of the House of Lords whose red-headed son was one of Tiger's cronies. Other constant visitors included Marie Corelli, the novelist, Dr. and Mrs. Ormiston Chant who lived close by and who had three attractive daughters with whom Tiger, in his sedater moments, used to sing part-songs.

Mrs. Chant was an indomitable social and temperance reformer and pacifist. She sometimes brought her American counterpart with her, a Mrs. Carrie Nation who made it her mission to go round her own country smashing up saloons with a hatchet. Mrs. Chant was not so destructive, but once she armed herself with a horsewhip and drove out the prostitutes who were displaying their charms in the promenade of the old Empire Theatre in Leicester Square. But this was a good many years later, after Tiger was grown up.

Tiger admired Mrs. Chant's bellicose spirit and ignored her pacifist views. He was only just in his teens and was as ardent as any of the imperialists who came to see his father—such people as Dr. Jameson, whose Raid is part of South Africa's history, Cecil Rhodes, Baden-Powell. Most of their achievements

B   7

still lay ahead of them. But Tiger has always been, and still is, extremely responsive to atmosphere and I am sure they helped to instil into him his life-long and bitter contempt for what we now call 'Safety First'.

'My God!' he wrote, some years before World War II, 'what a hopeless and sloppy slogan! What a fine thing to drum into the heads of our budding manhood! Do, please, be careful, men dear! You may get shot! Or run over! No wonder people get heart attacks.'

His own slogan, based on his youthful contacts and predilections, is:

'Live dangerously! It's the cowards who get killed!'

To which he sometimes adds: 'You can't fear God and danger, too!'

When he goes into a pub—which is every day he has enough cash to pay for other people's drinks as well as his own—he is quite capable of raising his glass in the ancient, and almost forgotten, pre-atomic toast:

'Here's to women and gunpowder! One brought me into the world and t'other'll probably take me out of it. I love the smell of both. Gentlemen, the Queen!'

Tiger's parents kept open house at 64 Gower Street. Men and women of all shades of opinion, not merely the bellicose, were welcome to refresh themselves at the long table, filled with cold food of every description, which ran the whole length of one of the walls in the dining-room. Visitors just 'dropped in'. And when they had finished eating (and drinking—mostly claret), they would repair to the drawing-room and hold what Rosa calls 'brains trusts' on every subject under the sun. She used to hide herself away on a stool as nearly as possible out of sight. She adds that Tiger kept quite out of sight. He was more at home with his catapult and pea-shooter. I am obliged to put on record that he gained his proficiency in these weapons, not by bombarding Georgina, but by peppering old gentlemen's legs.

Mr. Sarll, in his lighter moments, used to take out his revolver and betake himself to his private shooting gallery which was seventy feet long and ran through the cellar under the street. There he performed such feats as shooting out the flame of a candle held by a trembling and under-sized boy of sixteen with the improbable name of Bysouth.

Mr. Sarll insisted on Rosa's learning to shoot as well as Tiger, who, by the time he was twelve, could hit the rim of a penny at fifteen paces and shoot the ash off his father's cigar at twenty paces. Even after he had lost the sight of an eye, he won a cup which the Press Rifles used to shoot for on Leith Hill.

Tiger insists that his father always smoked an inferior brand of cigar when he encouraged his son to shoot off the ash. He belonged to an era in which it was regarded as almost sacrilegious to knock off the ash from a good cigar. It had to drop—preferably on the carpet to discourage moths. So Tiger thinks the trick must have been performed on some rather fruity Burmah cheroots his father kept for his less discriminating guests. Tiger himself became addicted to these at the age of six, though not as targets—by that time he was already a veteran smoker. When he was four, his parents inadvertently left a box of fifty Turkish cigarettes lying on a table when they went out. Tiger had chain-smoked the lot by the time they got back—and with no ill effects except that he has smoked like a chimney ever since.

Another of Mr. Sarll's recreations was music. He had his own organ at 64 Gower Street and occasionally he even deputized for the organists at Westminster Abbey and St. Paul's Cathedral. Tiger's paternal grandfather was a musician too who had helped the Rev. John Curwen develop the tonic sol-fa system of notation and who conducted a choir of three thousand when the new method was being introduced to the musical world many years before Tiger was born.

Tiger himself has never flown so high. But he has sung to a lady-love, and to others, to both the guitar and the mandolin. He still does. He is also conversant with the recorder, trumpet, bugle and, of course, the mouth organ with which he has enlivened many a route march. He still has the one he used during the Boer War. Its operative section is six inches long. I have heard him play many of the same tunes on his other mouth organ which must be the smallest in the world: its length is exactly one inch.

Mr. Sarll was almost as proud of his aquarium as of his

9

organ. Lord Randolph Churchill brought young Winston to see it one day. But Winston perversely was much more interested in the organ—or possibly in Rosa who took him to see it. Tiger himself was still in his cradle. He did not meet Winston till the Boer War.

When Tiger's already long legs acquired long trousers, he moved from Highfield School, Clifton, where he met Mrs. Besant, to Ongar Grammar School in Essex, where one of the older boys, a notorious bully, decided that Tiger, being a new boy, should be taught his place. So he whipped his fist against Tiger's chin as part of the first lesson.

The blow caught Tiger unawares. He toppled over backwards and banged his head so hard against the stone pathway they were standing on that he was out cold for several minutes. After he recovered, he soon came to the conclusion that he was too inexperienced to try to get his own back. So he went to the gym master and said:

'Please, sir, I want to learn boxing but I don't want anybody to know about it.'

Secrecy was made easier by the fact that Tiger has always loathed cricket and was not greatly attracted by football from which the gym master proceeded to get his pupil excused. Tiger paid for the lessons himself out of his pocket money which was always augmented considerably because, when he went back to school, his father used to look furtively over his shoulder, slip a sovereign into his hand and whisper: 'Don't tell your mother.' His mother did exactly the same except that she said: 'Don't tell your father.' Needless to say, Tiger obeyed them both implicitly at such times though not by any means at others.

After two terms, tuition in the noble art, Tiger went up to the bully, who was four years older than he was, much broader and somewhat shorter, told him what he was going to do and then did it, to everyone's satisfaction except the bully's.

Tiger was twelve by this time and, physically speaking, already an adult as he showed by tackling a burglar who was prowling about inside his parents' house. Tiger, whose bedroom was on the ground floor, woke to hear strange noises coming from the neighbourhood of the precious aquarium. He crept out into the hall and then up the stairs pulling a Turkish scimitar from its scabbard on the wall as he went past.

When he got to the landing, he dimly saw a strange man dressed from head to foot in skin-tight black and brought the scimitar down with all his strength on the intruder's shoulder without stopping to reflect that the man might easily have fallen apart in two slices as a result—Tiger was already at twelve as strong as a young carthorse. But his motto throughout life has always been: 'Hit first! You may never have another chance.' He has sometimes been caught napping, but his opponents have so far not been able to hit hard enough.

On this occasion, either Tiger himself did not hit hard enough or, much more probably, he happened quite by chance to use the flat of the blade instead of its cutting edge. He at once dropped his weapon and grappled with the man in black. They wrestled for a few moments to the accompaniment of loud screams from Mrs. Sarll and a servant on the landing above. Then the burglar managed to slip from Tiger's grasp—Tiger says the tights had been smeared with grease. But the man lost his balance and crashed through the balustrade falling fifteen feet to the stone floor below.

The aquarium went through the window on to a rockery. It was made of glass and was full of fish, aquatic plants, sand and three gallons of water.

The man was up and away in a flash. By the time Tiger got down the stairs, he had burst his way through a stained-glass window and vanished into the darkness. Tiger, returning unsuccessful from the chase, found his mother and the servant discussing how to get the aquarium upstairs again. It was quite undamaged. So were the contents except that about a gallon of water had slopped over on to the jagged stones of the rockery.

A few weeks later, Tiger reached his teens and went back to school. He soon decided, however, that he despised the masters (except the gym master), disliked most of the boys and loathed the food. So, one morning, instead of going to the classroom, he walked out of the gate and went on walking till he got home, a matter of about twenty-five miles.

I doubt if his parents were very surprised. And possibly the head master was relieved. At any rate, Tiger was not sent back to Ongar. He had, in fact, finished with school altogether, for his father engaged a special tutor for him, a Major Dobson, to coach him for Sandhurst.

Tiger was delighted. After weighing from the age of four the comparative attractions of bus conductor, fireman, explorer, naturalist, sailor and soldier, he finally decided in favour of the Army when he was ten.

Florence Nightingale was largely responsible. Tiger's mother had sent him to her on some errand he has forgotten. He found Miss Nightingale sitting up in bed, propped with pillows, in a room at the top of a long white marble staircase. She had large, brilliant eyes which looked right through him as she said:

'You are a nice, upright boy. You ought to be a soldier.'

From that moment, Tiger thought so too.

But, under Major Dobson, he soon found that it was the practical side of soldiering that appealed to him, not learning about it from text books. He learnt some things easily, especially if they were about natural history. He was good at mathematics, and chess—much less good at languages, though he learnt to speak Spanish quite well in after years. But the books he really liked were not text books. Daniel Defoe and Captain Marryat were his favourite authors. To him, Robinson Crusoe, Peter Simple, Mr. Midshipman Easy and the heroes of Marryat's more virile books (especially *The Pirate and Three Cutters*) were real people.

Tiger, in fact, was a product of the Naughty Nineties when youth was much more harum-scarum, tough, even wild, than we are accustomed to at the end of the Flabby Fifties of the twentieth century. Imperialism was the fashion—almost a religion—not a much misused and misinterpreted term of abuse. And Tiger was a man of fashion in more ways than one.

The gangs of his youth were not mere teddy boys a few of whom sometimes kicked over the traces. They were real thugs. The Seven Dials Gang operated only a few stones-throw from where he lived in aristocratic Bloomsbury. Farther afield there were many others: the Waterloo Road Gang; the New Cut Gang; the Stepney and Whitechapel Gangs; the Kingsland Road Gang to name just a few of those Tiger remembers. Each had its own jealously-guarded frontiers. Pitched battles be-tween them were frequent, with such weapons as bludgeons, stones, brickbats, weighted belts, broken bottles; and each gang had its girl members who egged the male ruffians on.

Tiger and his friends did not form a gang in any sense of the word. But they did often operate as a unit, partly for self-protection and partly because young people enjoy being in one another's company. Most of them were the sons of well-to-do 'Forsytes' in the neighbourhood—the professional people who had not yet deserted Bloomsbury for the suburbs. Some of them bore well-known names and attained eminence in various walks of life, so perhaps they had better remain anony-mous. Some of their juvenile escapades are scarcely in keeping with the staid respectability they acquired later.

In their extreme youth, Tiger and his friends never went out without their pea-shooters and catapults and it can be assumed that the targets were always human ones because Tiger would have fallen tooth and nail on anyone who shot at a cat or a dog or bird. One form of 'O.J. baiting'—O.J. being short for Old Josser—was to take one's iron hoop up to the top of such places as Hazelwood Hill and bowl it down full tilt with the deliberate intention of surreptitiously entangling it with an Old Josser's legs *en route*.

Tiger was only six when the Jack the Ripper crimes terrified the women of London. Hearing his parents discussing a report that 'Jack' used to chalk his initials on the doors of his intended victims, Tiger armed himself with a piece of chalk and wrote J.T.R. on his own back door with the result that none of the female servants would leave the house without escort for several weeks. In high glee, Tiger and his friends repeated the experi-ment elsewhere with equal success. And for some months afterwards, they used to sneak up behind any woman they found hurrying home at dusk and when close enough groan and shriek to see if she shrieked too. She generally did.

They were a little older, but not much, when they got hold of a pot of 'printer's varnish' which, Tiger says, was 'about ten times as sticky as bird-lime' and smeared it after dark over the bottom step of a house belonging to a 'fat, fussy, bad-tempered old bachelor' who lived alone and had a pretty housemaid of about nineteen, known to Tiger and his friends as 'Fatty', not because of her figure but because of her legs.

Having baited the trap, the conspirators rang the front door bell and retired hastily out of sight. Fatty duly opened the door and, seeing no one, shut it again.

She had scarcely had time to get back to the kitchen when the bell rang again—with an additional double rat-tat-tat on the knocker for fuller measure.

This time, Fatty came right out.

'Drat them young varmints,' she said loudly, adding as she walked down the steps towards the pavement: 'I'll larn them.'

When she trod on the bottom step, first one foot stuck and then the other. As she tried to wrench them free, she slipped and fell and, in another moment, both her hands were stuck too. Then her skirt plastered itself in a jumble round her waist revealing to the delighted boys what were termed in those days her 'unmentionables'. Finally, the crusty old bachelor came out to see why she was screaming. He got stuck too.

Tiger and the other young varmints, weeping with suppressed laughter, slipped away before retribution, in the shape of a patrolling bobby, overtook them. They were never caught but 'the Law' kept majestic watch for the flown birds for several weeks.

Such escapades were not meant to be cruel. They were simply Victorian youth's idea of fun. Tiger certainly did not mean any harm to Rosa when he emptied dozens of black-beetles into her bed just before her bedtime. He himself had no horror of black-beetles—quite the contrary.

Rosa undressed, unconscious of the fact that her bed was already tenanted. When she turned back the blankets, she screamed. Tiger was genuinely surprised that neither she nor his parents thought it funny.

A good many of Tiger's peccadilloes were due to the fact that he was bored. When he went to stay with his grandfather at St. Leonards, he was made to go to church each Sunday morning and sit through the whole service which included a full hour of quite unintelligible sermon. The family pew was one of the old high-walled boxes, so Tiger, aged six or seven,

used to fill his pockets with snails and set them to race one
another along the floor. Or he and a boy friend smuggled in
mice and played with them—until one escaped and got into
the next pew where the women occupants raised such a hulla-
baloo that the two culprits took to their heels and bolted out
of the church.

Tiger admits to having made many mistakes in his life but
this is one of the few he ever regretted.

'If we had stayed where we were,' he says, 'nobody would
have known where the mice came from.'

As Tiger and his friends grew older, they gradually discarded their childish amusements in favour of such things as
single-stick combats in their back gardens, and the still more
popular physical jerks, ju-jitsu, judo, boxing and fencing some
of which they practised at the Polytechnic and some at
Stemple's Gymnasium in Albany Street, near Regent's Park,
where an additional attraction was Stemple's daughter, Daisy,
who looked like a buxom sylph in her tight-fitting gym dress.
Tiger and his friends admired Daisy from afar. But neither
she nor any other girl had any part in their corporate activities.

When Tiger reached the age of fourteen, he found another
outlet for his embarrassingly abundant energies by joining the
Queen's Westminster (Volunteer) Regiment. According to the
rules, he was four years too young to be anything but a bugler.
But he was amply big enough physically. Indeed, the first time
he put on his uniform and jumped into a hansom to go to the
parade ground, the spike of his helmet went through the roof.
He soon showed that he could march, and of course shoot,
with the best. He was one of the team which won the Pascoe
Glyn Marching and Shooting Competition three years running.

The only thing he did not like about the Queen's Westminsters was the fact that the Commanding Officer, Colonel
Sir Howard Vincent, was a firm believer in spit and polish.
Nothing really satisfied Tiger in those days but action, almost
any kind of action, military or otherwise, except squarebash-
ing.

About the same time that he joined the Queen's Westminsters, Tiger heard of an organization called The Balloon
Club, the members of which clubbed together to hire balloons

—much as their sons and daughters (and grandchildren) do with gliders.

Tiger was too young, and had not got enough money, to join the Club, so he did the next best thing—he went to see them fly.

He remembers, very vividly indeed, that the balloonists asked the bystanders to hang on to the gondola to prevent the balloon from soaring away on its own after the mooring ropes had been cast off. Tiger, of course, was among those who responded and he immediately became so fascinated at the sight of the various clocklike instruments inside that instead of just hanging on with his hands, he leant his long body over the edge of the gondola. The crew was inside it by this time and when the order to let go was given, he did not hear it.

Suddenly his whole inside seemed to be dropping out of him and he glanced over his shoulder to see why. He found himself looking down into a sea of hundreds of little pigmies with comical little white upturned pigmy faces staring at his dangling legs from a very long way off and growing rapidly smaller.

And this time he did not even have his father's umbrella to help him rejoin them.

'Hell!' said a voice just above him. Then a hand grabbed his collar and he was hauled aboard.

There were three men in the gondola and Tiger learnt in due course that the one who had hauled him in was the Hon. C. S. Rolls whose name speaks for itself. By his side was a man with a pointed naval beard whose name was Captain Spenser, another of the pioneers in the new science of aeronautics. Tiger does not know who the third man was.

He explained what had happened and apologized. They all laughed, so Tiger laughed too and said:

'Won't my people be surprised when I get home tonight and tell them where I have been!'

The chap with a beard replied:

'You won't see your people tonight. You'll be lucky if you see them for six months. We're on a non-stop flight to the Andes. In South America, you know.'

Tiger, as it happened, did know. Also he believed what

Captain Spenser said and was utterly thrilled. He went on believing till he heard someone call:

'Hi, there! You young shaver! Tip that bag of ballast over the side. Hurry! We don't want to come down on top of those chimneys.'

He tipped it over, bag and all.

'My God!' Rolls said. 'Don't you realize those bags cost money? We can't afford to just chuck them away like that. Besides, you went and dropped it on a nursemaid who was wheeling a perambulator with a child in it and you've killed both of them. Next time, merely tip the sand out and smother them.'

The balloon came down shortly afterwards and its three legitimate occupants shook hands with Tiger before deflating the balloon so that it could be put on a train and taken back to base. They tactfully refrained from telling him that his weight (then about fifteen stone) had probably shortened their trip by about a hundred miles.

Tiger, for his part, with more low cunning than tact, refrained from telling his parents where he had been. He knew they would order him never to go near a balloon again and he had every intention of doing so at the first opportunity, whether his parents forbade him or not.

Actually, he was too heavy and his new friends discouraged him. But Rolls seems to have taken a fancy to him and taught him to drive a motor car—at the Crystal Palace and the Agricultural Hall where he was helping to run the first two Motor Shows ever held in London. This was in the summer of 1899 when Tiger was not quite seventeen and when cars had only recently emerged from the indignity of being classed with steam-rollers which meant that they were forbidden to use the roads unless they were preceded by a man on foot carrying a red flag. Even so, the English pioneers were luckier than Markus in Vienna who built a motor car with an internal combustion engine in 1875 and was banned from the streets after his first ride because of the noise. The Markus car was never taken on to the road again till seventy-five years later when it was still capable of doing a good five miles an hour. When I last saw it, it was standing just outside its home in the municipal museum near the Schönbrunn Palace.

17

Though Tiger was one of the first people in England to learn to handle a motor car and still drives a somewhat battered specimen along the highways and byways of Essex, he has always much preferred horses. He started to ride at about the same time as he started to smoke—when he was four. And in 1899, nearly thirteen years later, he still revelled in the sound of galloping hooves pulling a fire engine along the streets while the firemen yelled 'Hi! Hi! Hi!' at the top of their voices instead of clanging a bell as they do nowadays.

There was a fire station not very far from where he lived and whenever he heard the familiar sounds he used to leap on to the bicycle his father had given him as a reward for having tackled the burglar and pedal hell-for-leather to the scene of the fire behind the engine and its two grey horses, for whom he used to carry apples and sugar among the indispensable odds and ends in his various pockets.

Almost better than fire engines, however, were the four-wheeled skeleton carriages, painted yellow and black (like the first taxi-cabs), which could be seen, less than sixty years ago, dashing along the streets east of Regent's Park behind a pair of horses with one man sitting up high holding the reins and two more underneath on a bar, ready to jump off and rush to the horses' heads if they got out of hand.

Just what constituted 'getting out of hand' is not clear. Tiger says that at one moment the horses would be pawing the air and at the next might be almost standing on their heads. Sometimes they dashed along at breakneck speed: sometimes they backed vigorously when the driver wanted them to go forwards: sometimes they just pranced up and down, marking time, as it were, before deciding which wrong way to go next.

A good deal of the charm, in fact, lay in the delicious uncertainty which enveloped their every movement.

What were they doing? Merely being broken in—close by, and sometimes actually on, the busy Hampstead, Euston and Tottenham Court Roads where rival horse bus companies still indulged in cut-throat competition—buses with knife-edged, uncovered seats on top and a place for one passenger next to the driver. Tiger always took this seat if he could because he and the drivers spoke the same language so far as horses were concerned and he liked their Cockney wit when the traffic got into a tangle, which it frequently did—almost as much as it does now.

As the jogging years gradually outstripped such things, Tiger's mother died, quite suddenly. This was in 1899, when she was only forty-six and Tiger and Rosa respectively sixteen and twenty. Rosa could not believe she was dead and, seeing her lying so calm and so peaceful, but so cold to the touch, in her open coffin, carried hot water bottles up from the kitchen to lay beside her and waken her with their friendly warmth.

Tiger, by that time, had given up the idea of trying to pass into Sandhurst and was training to become a doctor. I do not think he ever really intended to practise, but the failure of the medical profession to save his mother's life made him even less inclined than ever.

He found solace among his comrades in the Queen's Westminsters. That summer, they took part in manœuvres near Aldershot under the command of General Sir Redvers Buller. During the last forty-eight hours, they marched the whole of one day and well into the night along roads which were so dusty that Tiger could scarcely see the man in front of him. His water bottle got itself mixed up with a gun limber—it was one of those glass contraptions covered with grey felt which were standard equipment in those days. And he had toothache.

At the end of the forced march, the regiment was deployed and ordered to lie down in icy-cold, dew-drenched heather to wait for the order to attack which did not come till midnight.

While I was rummaging in Tiger's papers sixty years afterwards, I found a notebook in which he said he had never been so happy in his life.

Two months later, the Boer War started. It was a conflagration exactly to Tiger's taste. He made a dash for his bicycle the moment he heard the news and pedalled frantically to see Sir Howard Vincent.

'When does the regiment start, sir?' he asked.

2. INVALIDED OUT

STARTING proved less easy than either Tiger or Sir Howard anticipated. An impeccably dressed sportsman at the War Office told Sir Howard (in effect) that it was very patriotic, and all that, of the Queen's Westminsters to offer themselves for service.

'But the fact is, old man,' he went on, 'we've already got far more men than we need. After all, they're only Boers, you know. Just farmers. They haven't got a chance against our Johnnies. We'll be in, what's the name of the place?—Pretoria —in a couple of months.'

Sir Howard went back, crestfallen, to Buckingham Gate where the entire regiment was waiting in not at all absent-minded, empire-building enthusiasm. They heard him in silence and then went gloomily home.

Later on, some of them joined the City Imperial Volunteers —the C.I.V. But it was not the same thing. The Queen's Westminsters were already a team; the C.I.V. wasn't.

Tiger was one of the few who were in no mood to wait a day.

'If they won't take the regiment, sir,' he told Sir Howard, 'I'll go out on my own and enlist when I get there. Some of our chaps are bound to be killed. Even if they are only fighting Boers. And I'll be on the spot to take their place.'

Sir Howard heartily approved. But Mr. Sarll told his son not to be a fool.

'What about your medical studies, my boy?' he asked. 'You know what the War Office told Sir Howard: "Over in two months." Before you even get to Cape Town. It will be impossible to get a passage home. You'll be kicking your heels out there doing nothing except spend money for at least six months. Utter folly, I call it. I never heard such nonsense.'

Tiger argued but his father refused to change his mind— possibly (as Tiger now believes) because he could not bear to think of his son having all the fun while he himself had to stay at home.

So Tiger had to finance his expedition mainly out of his

pocket money which was ample for most purposes but not for fitting out a young blood of the nineteenth century about to embark on a career as a soldier. He bought himself a sword from Wilkinson's and a rifle as well as a revolver (with plenty of ammunition) from Cogswell & Harrison.

He still has the revolver, but not the rifle, and the sword has been replaced by a sword-stick without which, even today, he would feel improperly dressed.

His Uncle Tom advised him to take his own horse.

'Those War Office wallahs,' Uncle Tom declared, 'don't know a horse from a hay-rick. Besides, you need one which is up to your weight. I'll tell you what: why not take that chestnut of mine? You're used to one another and I don't need him. I only wish I were young enough to go with you. Mind you give them a good thrashing!'

Tiger modestly undertook to do his best and accepted the horse with enthusiasm. It was a fine animal—so fine, in fact, that nothing but the best would be good enough for it on the voyage.

Which meant that Tiger himself would have to go steerage because he had already spent almost all the money he had in the world on his equipment.

So he went steerage and it was just as well for he learnt, for the first time, that the true adventurer is generally impecunious so that he at once found himself among kindred spirits, all as fighting-mad as he was—a mixed lot by the class standards in which he had been brought up, but blood brothers in outlook and temperament.

The boat was the *Garth Castle* of 9000 tons and she sailed from Southampton on 11th November 1899. She was not one of the ocean greyhounds and carried sails as well as steam engines and her maximum speed which she seldom tried to attain was twelve knots. It took her seven weeks to get to Cape Town so that, by War Office calculations, the war ought to have been over long before Tiger arrived.

The kindred spirits who numbered about twenty, had no wireless to reassure them so they relieved their anxiety, and their pent-up blood pressure, by blowing off steam in any way that came handy. At Las Palmas, for instance, they all went on shore. Tiger joined forces with a red-headed lawyer named Crowther who took him to what he heard call for the first time, a 'knocking shop'. Two naked girls planted themselves on his knees. Their nakedness did not embarrass him but their behaviour did and Crowther appears to have found his couple equally distasteful. Crowther paid, through the nose, for two bottles of bad champagne and then he and Tiger got up to leave.

This did not suit the proprietress, or the girls, and two negroes tried to bar their way to the door. Tiger knocked out one and Crowther soon dealt with the other; then they rushed headlong down a marble staircase towards the street.

Tiger's equipment included a telescope which he had bought to help him spot Boers and he took it with him everywhere to make sure it was not stolen. On this occasion, he wrapped his long legs round it on the stairs and slithered the rest of the way to the bottom on his head. He was not hurt, but the telescope carried a permanent kink for the rest of its life.

In process of time the kindred spirits went back to the quayside and hailed the boatmen who had beguiled them with an offer to take them ashore for 'only one shilling, mister'. They now demanded a pound a head to put them back on board. None of the other boatmen would take them for less so, in the end, they had to pay—in advance.

But one of the party decided to get at least a bit of his own back and, as Tiger was clambering up the rope ladder, he heard shots. Someone, and he is still not prepared to say who, had drilled six holes in one of the boats with his revolver.

The boatmen jabbered and shouted in Portuguese and shook their fists as they rowed hurriedly back to the quay where they went straight to the harbour police who sent a launch to fetch the 'criminal' back under arrest. The captain of the *Garth Castle* pulled up the rope ladder and swore he would let no 'bloody foreigner' come aboard his ship. But he changed his mind when the launch was followed by a Portuguese gunboat, and very soon the kindred spirits were being interrogated by an irate Portuguese officer.

Having failed to get a word out of any of them, the officer told the captain he must on no account leave until the matter had been cleared up and then went back to consult the Chief of Police. It was getting dark by this time so, as soon as the gunboat had disappeared into the haze, the *Garth Castle* made off hastily towards the open sea.

I think the Portuguese authorities must have secretly been relieved. The boatmen themselves had suffered no damage and it cannot have cost them more than a few pence to plug the holes. But if it had happened today, the world's Press would have made an international incident out of it.

Two days after leaving Las Palmas, the passengers on the *Garth Castle* saw what Tiger still insists was a sea-serpent. He pooh-poohed my suggestion that it might have been a line of dolphins leaping out of the water.

'It is quite true that only bits of its back were visible—rather like the teeth of a huge saw,' he declared. 'But I'm absolutely certain that each piece was part of one animal. We could see it quite plainly. It was less than a mile away. The captain altered course to try to get nearer, but it took fright and disappeared. I believe he entered it in his log, but of course I do not know for certain.'

One of the steerage passengers not admitted to the band of kindred spirits was a German businessman who rashly boasted one day that it was his custom to enjoy a woman three times a week.

'You must feel very lonely here, all by yourself,' somebody commiserated when the story got around.

'Too true,' the German murmured.

'Well, you needn't be,' the other said. 'There's a beautiful young widow on board who is as lonely as you are. Would you like to be introduced?'

The German intimated that he was not merely willing, but eager—as well as able. So the go-between sought out the 'widow' who was actually a fresh-faced youth of nineteen, named Percival, whose co-operation had been arranged in advance. It included his answering to the name of Madeline.

The conspirators arrayed 'Madeline' suitably and bribed a steward to install 'her' in the top berth of an empty cabin. Then they ushered the German in, closed the door and waited eagerly outside for developments.

The suitor found the 'lady' unexpectedly coy. Instead of welcoming him with open arms, 'she' slapped his face when he tried to climb into the bunk. In the end, he had to retire, unsatisfied and disgruntled, but still in ignorance of the hoax.

The next day, the conspirators 'arrested' him and hauled him before a very real-looking Court of Inquiry at which one of the ship's officers deputized for the captain. The 'widow' having given evidence (dressed in 'weeds'), the unfortunate German was found guilty and sentenced to pay £2 to each of the stewards. Tiger insists that he never discovered that he had been hoaxed.

Having disposed of its first case, the Court decided to carry on with its hilarious work. To Tiger's consternation, he was the next to be arraigned.

The prosecutor—he was Crowther, by the way—asked him: 'Did you visit a house of ill-fame while ashore at Las Palmas? Did you have a telescope with you? What did you expect to see with it? Was its purpose, in fact, to enable you to observe yourself sitting in the house aforesaid with a naked girl on each knee? Did you, on leaving the establishment after an indecent interval, assault two members of its staff with the telescope and thereby render it unfit for use in the service of your Queen and country?'

Tiger, feeling rather sheepish, pleaded guilty and was sentenced by acclamation to be keel-hauled. But the sentence was ultimately commuted, after further hilarity, to an extra ducking when they crossed the Line a few days later.

One of the kindred spirits on his way to have a crack at the Boers was an American named Joe Lyons. He was about Rosa's height, which was five feet two inches, had a thin, wizened face which looked like parchment and had been a scout with Buffalo Bill, besides claiming to have acted as escort to the fabulous Pony Post of the days of the Indian wars. Officially, Lyons admitted to being fifty-two. But after a few drinks, he would sometimes confess to a pal that he was 'something over seventy'.

Tiger had actually met Buffalo Bill, though he was only five when the famous American came to see if what he had heard about Mr. Sarll's skill with a revolver was true. Before he went away, he gave Tiger a revolver which he said had belonged to Kit Carson, the almost legendary hero of so many 'Western' adventure stories. The revolver is another of Tiger's many treasures.

In such circumstances, it was natural that Tiger and Lyons took to one another at once. Both were under the spell of the same heroes. Both were fascinated by danger and bored by security and safety first. Indeed, both were only fully alive when face to face with sudden death.

Long before the *Garth Castle* reached Cape Town, the kindred spirits agreed that they would offer themselves for enlistment, not as individuals but as a unit. Some of them were veterans; all had some training and all knew how to ride, though only Tiger had brought his own horse.

'It's all of us, or none,' they promised one another. 'They must take us as a troop, or not at all. And that goes for you, too, you damned old Methuselah,' they added to Lyons with the usual embellishments.

'Supposing the war's over,' mused a pessimist. 'What do we do then?'

'Start another one, you fool,' declared some swashbuckler. 'Like that chap Jameson.'

They all laughed except Tiger who loves getting into trouble but prefers not to start it, and who had also met Jameson.

In those pre-wireless days, the kindred spirits did not know whether they had been chasing a wild goose till the *Garth Castle* actually docked at Cape Town. The fire-eaters let out a cheer when they found that, from their standpoint, all was well.

In fact, the war was so very far from being over, that when they marched, in fours, into Rosebank Camp, the recruiting officer, a Major Villiers, was extremely relieved to see them.

'It's all of us, or none, sir,' Crowther told him. 'We're offering for the South African Light Horse. As a troop. One of us,' he added, pointing out Tiger, 'has his own horse.'

'Can you all ride?' Major Villiers inquired. 'And can you shoot?'

'Yes,' they chorused.

'You'll have to prove it, of course, before I accept you,'

Major Villiers warned them. 'And there's another thing: that man there. He's too old.'

'I'm not,' Lyons declared indignantly. 'I'm only fifty-two. Not a day older.'

'Frankly, I don't believe you,' Major Villiers replied. 'Any more than I believe that boy over there'—he pointed at Tiger—'is old enough. The regulations say I must not accept anyone under eighteen or over thirty-five.'

'We don't take the Queen's shilling without them,' Crowther declared. 'Isn't that so, men?'

They chorused as before.

Major Villiers considered the matter dubiously for a moment. Then his face cleared.

'Very well,' he told them. 'As a troop, you are entitled to a non-combatant cook. And I admit I would have taken young Sarll for eighteen if he had not rashly put seventeen down on the form. Now, off you go, the lot of you.'

Tiger and Lyons, respectively the long and the short of the troop, as well as its youngest and oldest members, led the field in the shooting tests. Actually, when Tiger enlisted, he could have hit the target with his revolver when holding it behind his back and aiming by looking into a mirror in front of him. But he only mentioned this accomplishment to Lyons.

Both passed the riding tests with ease, too, Lyons on a little Basuto pony and Tiger on his chestnut which stood a good couple of hands higher than any other horse in the S.A.L.H. Indeed, it was such an outstanding animal that a major asked Tiger to let him have it. Tiger, being no more than a trooper, had to say 'yes', and also had to take a tiny Basuto pony instead, scarcely big enough to keep his feet off the ground. It was no consolation that the major had the chestnut shot under him a few days later. At the end of the war, Tiger received £37. 10. 0. compensation for the loss of the horse. His own estimate of its value was three hundred pounds.

The troop was posted to the South African Light Horse in which Tiger himself became Trooper Number 817. His C.O. was Colonel Byng.

Many years later, Tiger took his first wife to call on his old commanding officer who, by that time, was Field-Marshal Lord

Byng of Vimy. Lord Byng took Mrs. Sarll aside and said to her, but not in Tiger's hearing: 'I hope you are as proud of your husband as I am. He is one of the grandest soldiers I have ever met.'

The troop of the kindred spirits was sent from Cape Town to Durban on a ship called *The Jamaican*. But when they got on board, with their horses, they found that most of the crew, including all the stokers, had deserted because the Army offered them higher pay. So the troop had to turn to and take their place.

Tiger was naturally regarded as having the right physique for a stoker. He very soon began to wish he had been built on the Lyons scale. The more he shovelled, the more *The Jamaican*'s engines seemed to eat.

They were still many hours out from Durban when coal began to run short. They ripped up the deck, tore down all the woodwork in the cabins but they still had not enough fuel to take them into Durban harbour.

It was finally decided to hoist the horses over the side and drop them into the sea to swim for the shore. A boat was lowered to try to prevent the animals swimming out to sea by mistake and to frighten off prowling sharks.

All of them got ashore safely except three or four. The amateur crew then resumed their role as troopers. The front was not many miles away and they were very soon in the thick of the fighting.

Tiger was not long in realizing that the South African War was a very different affair from the mock battles he had engaged in on the moors near Aldershot. In fact, each of the many wars he has known has been different from all the others. Perhaps that was one of their charms: he had no idea what it was going to be like till he was in the thick of it.

There was a sort of breezy *camaraderie* about the South African War which appealed to Tiger from the start. Not too much formality; not too many rules; masses of individuality; not many useless sheets of paper to be filled with incomprehensible and infuriating figures.

Tiger, as we already know, provided much of his own equipment although he was merely one of the thousands of common,

27

absent-minded beggars whose weaknesses, according to Kipling, were so great that you had to take him as you found him. But he was expected to think, and act, for himself and often by himself and if he had been as absent-minded as all that he would not have survived to tell me his story.

I suppose the South African War was the last major conflict in which a commanding officer called out to his men (as Colonel Byng did one day): 'Ten pounds to the man who's first on top of that kopje!'

The S.A.L.H. were dismounted at that moment, somewhere not far from the Tugela River where one of the great battles of the war was fought, and a terrific scramble followed—ten pounds represented nearly six weeks' pay.

The race was won by Lyons, the seventy-year-old 'noncombatant' American 'cook'.

One of the junior officers in the S.A.L.H. was a sort of hybrid between combatant and civilian. His name was Winston Churchill who, besides being a lieutenant, was also, when occasion demanded, correspondent of the *Morning Post*. He was a dynamic, colourful young man who succeeded in falling foul of most people in the regiment but without arousing their animosity because it was obvious to everyone that he had guts.

Tiger remembers one rather hectic day, also on the Tugela, when he, as Number Three, was trying to hold seven horses under fire instead of the regulation three (plus his own) prescribed by the *Manual of Training*. Winston was kneeling, not far off, engaged in bandaging Trooper Jackson who had been wounded in the foot.

Tiger's hands were much too full for him to bother about either of them. Bullets were singing and crackling round him and one had just clipped the ear of one of the horses. The frightened beast reared, whinnied, snorted, plunged and tried to run away, causing the other seven to follow suit.

It is not easy to control one horse in such conditions, let alone seven, and Tiger decided that the only thing to do was to keep the beasts moving. So he started to walk them in a fairly large circle and had his back to Winston and Trooper Jackson when he heard a roar behind him:

'Where the hell d'you think you're going? Don't you know

there's a war on? Bring those damned brutes here. I've got to get this chap on to one of them.'

Tiger did his best and then resumed his circling while Winston got back to the war. Neither of them ever referred to the incident again. Nor did Tiger ever remind Winston that he had once been taken to see the Sarll aquarium in Bloomsbury. But they were in daily contact with one another until Ladysmith was relieved. Winston went back to England soon afterwards and became a Member of Parliament. Tiger went home too, about the same time. We shall see why in a few moments.

Tiger seems to have enjoyed himself helping Sir Redvers Buller relieve Ladysmith at least as much as he enjoyed the mock battle General Buller threw him into near Aldershot. It is true that he did not have toothache. But he certainly had plenty of other discomforts.

The army was short of food; the uniforms were unsuitable; most of the men had been given the wrong sort of training— when they had had any training at all. Most of the units stayed in the front line for months on end without ever being relieved. And they seldom had a chance to wash either themselves or their clothes.

One day, in the middle of a de-lousing session, Sir Redvers Buller himself happened to ride by. Everybody had his shirt off and all, except Tiger, were busy picking lice out of the seams in which they love to congregate.

Tiger was merely shaking his shirt vigorously to get the sand out. Sir Redvers reined in his horse and said:

'That's no use, my lad. I always turn my shirt inside out. And then use the dandy brush. Like this. After that, you go carefully over the seams and pick the rest out, one by one.'

Tiger did not like to tell his Commander-in-Chief that he had already searched the seams and not found a single louse. He is convinced that this was because he was a vegetarian.

A more likely explanation is that he was so tough that no louse could get its teeth into him.

A shell which burst almost at Tiger's feet during the battle of Colenso filled the back of his neck with shrapnel fragments some of which still emerge occasionally after being there for sixty years. As if this were not enough, the shell drove sand particles so deeply into his left eye that he has never been able to see with it again. His other eye was also damaged.

As soon as his eyes had been attended to he went back to duty. Not long afterwards, when he was helping to unload a gun-limber at a rail-head, it broke loose on the ramp and a wheel went over Tiger's feet as the gun charged down the slope.

'Better keep your boots on, son,' Lyons advised as Tiger writhed in agony. 'There ain't no use in taking 'em off till your feet can be attended to. The boots will hold the splayed bones in place till a doctor can set 'em.'

'They hurt like hell,' Tiger told him.

So Lyons poured a bottle of iodoform into each boot making the pain ten times worse but, Tiger supposes, helping to prevent gangrene as the days went past without his feet receiving any further attention.

He was still able to ride so he still did not report sick.

Another brief interval and a Boer bullet went through the fleshy part of his thigh, so near his groin that he thought at first that it had deprived him of his manhood. But it had not and he found he could still ride his pony so he carried on.

Rosa says, however, that he was not riding at the time the bullet struck him but walking on his splayed feet with a wounded man in his arms. Her authority is Mary Kingsley, a tall, fair, raw-boned woman, niece of Charles Kingsley, the writer, and herself the first woman explorer in West Africa. She gave Tiger his first snake when he was twelve and he fussed over it and overfed it so that it died, which left him inconsolable for days.

When the South African War started, Mary volunteered as a nurse. She wrote to Tiger's father to say he had been recommended for the V.C. It is quite possible—we know what Colonel Byng thought of him—but by rights Mary Kingsley should not have known. Tiger himself denies it, but he had no more right to know than Mary Kingsley had. All that can be said for certain, therefore, is that he did not get it.

Tiger, one-eyed, lame and weary, held on grimly until Ladysmith was relieved. And, when he rode into the town, through the assembled Gordon Highlanders who were too weak to stand to welcome their deliverers, what worried him most was the fact that he had ridden completely through the seat of his riding breeches.

As he rode past, a nurse ran up to him and urged him to dismount.

'We've got some nice soup in the tent over there,' she told him. 'You look as if you need it.'

'What sort of soup is it?' Tiger asked, surreptitiously feeling to find out just how bare his backside really was.

'Horse,' the nurse said.

'No, thanks,' Tiger replied. 'I'm a vegetarian.'

He rode on and that night he managed to cobble a patch on somehow. The next morning he reported sick.

They had to cut his boots off and his lacerated toes were stuck so firmly to the leather that they had to cut the flesh away too. Yet he considers he was lucky; he did not have to have his toes amputated. Not only were there very few surgeons in the British Army in those days, but practically no anaesthetics. When a limb was amputated the usual practice was to stop the bleeding by searing the wound with a red-hot blacksmith's iron.

Tiger still has his legs and arms. Indeed, his feet recovered to such an extent that years later he entered for an international marathon race from Windsor to the White City sponsored by the *Evening News*. He was up in the very front when his friend, Vincent Smith—now a group captain living in Canada—tried to cool him down by throwing a bucket of water over him. He was so excited that he forgot to keep hold of the handle and the bucket caught Tiger on the chin knocking him out for ten minutes. But he finished the race.

The doctor who examined him in Ladysmith did not beat about the bush. After examining his eyes, he said:

'The right one will be all right if you wear glasses. But the other, no. The optic nerve is damaged. You will never be able to use the eye again.'

'Are you sure?' Tiger asked.

'Absolutely,' the doctor told him. 'I'm afraid your soldiering days are over. As soon as we have patched up your feet and legs, you will be interviewed by the Field Medical Board. No

31

doubt you will be discharged and they will give you a disability pension.'

'But I can see well enough with my other eye,' Tiger protested.

'You can't be a soldier with only one eye,' the M.O. maintained.

'What about Nelson?' Tiger asked.

'Nelson wasn't a soldier,' the M.O. pointed out, unanswerably.

While Tiger was in hospital, Mary Kingsley came to see him. She was nursing Boer prisoners of war at Simon's Bay in what is now Cape Province. Not long afterwards, she herself fell ill and then died. She was buried at sea and Tiger dropped a wreath into the water as her coffin slid below the surface.

Tiger still thinks of her as 'almost the only woman explorer who really did explore'. He has read all her books and heard much more about her adventures from her own lips. When she went to West Africa, it was still the darkest part of the Dark Continent—filled with malaria and mystery, sleeping sickness and sorcery, yellow fever and white ivory and it was rightly known as the White Man's Grave.

In due course, Tiger went before the Field Medical Board which duly invalided him out and offered him a pension. He refused it. When the Board asked why, he would not say. The Board argued with him and at last they compromised on a temporary pension of one shilling a day for two years, payable yearly. Then they sent him home—in a troopship this time—and at the Government's expense instead of his own.

Why would he not accept a pension? Because he did not accept the Board's verdict that he would never again be fit enough to soldier. So, he went home determined to prove the Board wrong.

Building up his strength again at 64 Gower Street, he fell foul of his neighbour, Mrs. Chant, who was a 'pro-Boer', as well as a bellicose pacifist. She not only called him a murderer but, when he retaliated by saying she was a traitor, threw a cup of scalding coffee in his face. Some of it went into his eyes. She was horrified by her own thoughtlessness and begged him to forgive her and they remained the best of friends.

In due course, Tiger considered that sufficient strength had come back to his limbs. And he had proved at his father's revolver range that he could shoot almost as well with one eye as with two.

Then he said good-bye to his father and Rosa, looked in with a twinkle in his serviceable eye to tell the Chants where he was going, which was to Southampton, to board the first boat for Cape Town.

3. BACK TO THE WAR

TIGER got back to Cape Town in May 1901. There were no kindred spirits with him this time and he had no horse. He still had his own revolver but he had found swords were not used so he had taken a swordstick instead. And he had decided that the British Government could supply him with a rifle and ammunition—assuming, of course, that it accepted his services.

As he went down the gangway, I am sure he looked quite confident though his heart ought to have been pretty near his mouth. He had journeyed some six thousand miles on the off chance that he could prove the medical authorities wrong in saying that he was of no further use to the Army. He had no idea how he was going to set about doing so. He only knew it would not be the slightest use going back to Rosebank Camp and trying to re-enlist in the South African Light Horse.

Then what was he to do?

As it turned out, he did not have to do anything. He had not got halfway down the gangway when he heard a rather cockney voice calling out:

'Anyone aboard want to join the British Army? Anyone aboard want to join the British Army? Anyone aboard——'

'Yes, I do,' Tiger said.

The recruiting sergeant looked him up and down, all six feet four inches of him, and remarked:

'That's the spirit, me lad. Come alonga me and I'll soon fix you.'

Within half an hour of landing, Tiger found himself a scout in Sir George Gorringe's Flying Column, a picked body of men whose job was to take the Boers on at their own game of small, self-sufficient units which attacked where they were least expected. Thanks in large measure to the American, Lyons, Tiger already knew the game pretty well. But he soon knew it better.

The recruiting sergeant asked no awkward questions and did not send him for a medical examination. Men were needed far too badly to worry about such matters.

34

Tiger started in the Flying Column as an ordinary trooper but he was very soon granted additional pay as a trained scout so that he received 12s. 6d. a day, nearly double what he had been getting in the South African Light Horse. But not long afterwards, the British Government announced its intention of disbanding the column which they regarded as an expensive luxury. When a millionaire, whose name was Abe Bailey, heard of the decision, he immediately offered to pay the Column's wage bill out of his own pocket so the Column was reprieved. Tiger is convinced that the war would have gone on for at least two years longer if Abe Bailey had not intervened.

Tiger was sent by train to De Aar, a station some four hundred miles north-east of Cape Town and not far from where what was then called Cape Colony joined what was the Orange Free State. It was a tedious and potentially dangerous journey mostly through wild, desolate country from which a hail of bullets could have swept the train at any hour of the day or night.

Actually, the only excitement Tiger encountered was when his train was waiting in a station and another train drew alongside coming from the opposite direction. As it braked to a standstill, Tiger heard loud gusts of laughter from a handful of Tommies standing on the platform.

At first he could not see anything to laugh at. Most of the people in the other train were nurses who had clustered round the apertures in the cattle trucks they were riding in and were waving to the men standing on the platform. They did not realize, and nor did Tiger at first, that the words 'Officers' Remounts' were chalked in large letters on their trucks. Tiger never discovered whether the words described the previous occupants of the trucks or had been put there by some wag after the nurses got in.

The guffaws brought a very dignified-looking matron from the station building. In 1941, she would probably have laughed too. But in 1901, she stiffened, turned round hastily and came back a few moments later with a native servant who carried a mop and bucket. The offending words were then expunged amid resounding cheers and some rather furtive giggles.

Tiger's life with Gorringe's Flying Column was in many ways reminiscent of the stories Lyons had told him about Buffalo Bill and Kit Carson. There were ambushes and sudden surprises, feats of individual bravery, alarms, excursions and a growing sense of admiration for a brave and skilful enemy.

You had to be on your guard all the time. Once when Tiger was out on a reconnaissance, by himself, he saw two men in British uniforms riding towards him.

'That's funny,' he remarked to himself, after looking at them through his telescope. 'I didn't know the Imperial Yeomanry were in this neighbourhood.'

The two men did not appear to have seen him, so he hid behind a rock, and waited for them. When they came nearer, he heard them talking to one another in Dutch. Evidently they had captured two of the Yeomanry and taken their uniforms.

Captain Young who commanded the special scouts decided to follow the two Boers and see if they led the column to larger quarry. He was a South African and, in spite of his vast girth, a champion runner, as well as quite fearless.

The two Boers were easy to track. One of their horses was unshod and the other had cast a shoe. The Flying Column scouts followed them for several days and then, one afternoon, they saw a number of men on horseback on the skyline a few miles ahead.

Tiger, looking at them through his telescope, said they were Boers. Sergeant Sampson, with his binoculars, declared that they could not be Boers because they were on the skyline. He was an Australian who had thrown up a good job 'down under' to strike a blow for the old country.

Tiger was quite certain that they were, but there was nothing further he could say, or do, about it, except keep his eye open.

Soon afterwards, the scouts entered a wide valley which closed in gradually and culminated in a 'saddle' known as Zaman Komst—apparently because it was the Meeting Place of the Hills. Presently Captain Young saw that the Boers were holding the hill to his right, so he sent three men to see if the hill to the left was occupied too.

The three men, all N.C.O.s, left their horses in charge of Trooper Kootze, who appears to have been a loyal Boer, and started to climb up the hillside on foot. They were already out of sight when Captain Young discovered that the Boers were also holding the saddle itself, so he ordered Tiger to hurry after the patrol and warn it to be careful.

As Tiger panted after them, he suddenly saw Corporal Athelstan rolling down the steep, rock-studded hillside. Tiger thought at first that he had simply lost his footing and he stood still for a moment wondering whether he ought to go to his help or deliver his message first.

Then a bullet zipped past his ear and ricocheted whiningly off a rock just behind him.

He dived quickly for cover and lay motionless for a moment while he tried simultaneously to work out what had happened and where the shot came from.

He saw Corporal Athelstan pick himself up at the bottom of the hill and dash off. But where were Sergeant Sampson and the New Zealander, Corporal Cox?

Tiger had only heard one shot so far—the one aimed at him. He inferred that Corporal Athelstan's two comrades had been taken by surprise and either captured or knocked on the head— or both.

But what was he to do in this case? Push on and see if he could effect a rescue? Stay where he was? Go back and report to Captain Young?

Corporal Athelstan would have done that already, he reflected, which left him with two alternatives. Before he had decided which to take, he saw a Boer coming cautiously towards him.

'I suppose he's coming to see whether they got me,' he decided, 'and whether I'm alone or with a reception party. Well, he isn't going to find out.'

As there was only one Boer, Tiger laid down his rifle and took his Cogswell & Harrison revolver out of its holster hoping it would not break if he brought its butt down on the Boer's head. Then he looked round cautiously to make sure no more Boers were trying to stalk him from his left. He could not see any, so he crouched down behind his rock, muscles tensed, ears alert and his one eye trained on the rock in front, ready to flash instantaneous instructions to his hands.

The Boer was inching his way forward, but, thanks in large measure to old Lyons, he was up against a man who knew at least as much about scouting as he did and he had no time to realize what hit him.

When he did not return, the leader of the commando rashly sent a second man to find out what had happened to the first. Meanwhile he kept the rest of his men under cover instead of pushing forward to seize the whole crest and surround the scouts who numbered about fifty, which Captain Young found later had been his original intention.

Bullets were flying in many directions by the time Tiger had dealt with the second Boer exactly as he had dealt with the first. Then he rolled their bodies down the hill in the wake of Corporal Athelstan. He joined in the firing, too, when he had done so, taking pot shots with his rifle at any Boer who showed himself. The Boers returned his fire and a spent bullet ricocheted off a rock into his arm but without doing any serious damage.

Presently he saw Trooper Kootze at the bottom of the hill leap on to his horse with bullets spitting into the dust all round him and gallop madly back towards the main body of Gorringe's Flying Column which was some ten miles behind. He was riding bareback and without a bridle. All he had to control his pony with was a halter—and his legs.

'There goes a brave man,' Tiger said to himself. 'By Jove, I wouldn't like to be in his shoes.'

Kootze reached the main body unscathed. Gorringe's men spurred their horses and the first shells from their two field guns, whistling unpleasantly close over Tiger's head, sent the Boer commando racing helter-skelter for safety.

Later Sir George Gorringe sent for Tiger and said:

'Trooper Sarll! Captain Young has told me what you did today and how you undoubtedly saved the advance guard from destruction. I have decided to recommend you for a commission.'

'But, sir,' Tiger stammered. 'I didn't do anything except lie behind a rock and fire my rifle when I saw a target. It was Trooper Kootze who saved the advance guard.'

'Trooper Kootze,' Gorringe replied, 'is under arrest. If you want to know why, it is because he deserted his post under fire. You, unless I have been misinformed, prevented the advance guard, single-handed, from being surrounded. There were between three and four hundred Boers on those hillsides.'

A good many years later, when Tiger and his wife were having dinner with Sir George Gorringe at his home in Shoreham, Tiger again raised the question of Trooper Kootze.

'You see, sir,' he said, 'I am the only person who saw what he did. The bullets were flying round him like hail. Instead of taking cover, he galloped back to the main body, regardless of the danger, riding bareback and without reins, only a halter. How he escaped being hit is a mystery. And it was a remarkable feat of horsemanship, too, sir. Only a brave man could have done it.'

'I don't see it like that,' Sir George said. 'He had received orders to guard his comrades' horses. But what did he do? He left the horses to take care of themselves thus failing in his duty to ensure his comrades' safety. In other words, he deserted his post. It was unpardonable.'

'But, sir,' Tiger persisted, 'if he had stayed where he was, his comrades would all have been killed. The scouts would have been wiped out.'

'You don't know that,' Sir George maintained. 'Nor do I. Nor did he. You have simply drawn an unjustifiable inference from something that never happened. The man had his orders. He disobeyed them. If he had taken the horses behind cover and tethered them before riding away, he might possibly have had a case. But he didn't. Have another glass of port?'

So far as I know, the battle of Zaman Komst does not figure in the official accounts of the South African War. But official accounts seldom show what war is like to those who actually fight it. And in this case there are not many survivors still able, like Tiger, to bring the bones of its history alive.

A battle means something different to each and every individual who fights in it. To Trooper Kootze it brought tragedy and a court-martial, which sentenced him to three years' imprisonment. To Sergeant Sampson and Corporal Cox it meant merciless ragging because they were ultimately rescued bound hand and foot, without a stitch of clothing and unhurt.

And to Trooper Sarll, the same battle meant a commission which he had a sneaking suspicion he didn't deserve.

But he is extremely proud of having received it.

He was gazetted a lieutenant on 28th October 1901 and ordered to report at once to the Border Scouts, having been with Gorringe roughly six months. The Border Scouts were mostly picked men of mixed African and European parentage for which reason they were generally known, irregularly but affectionately, as The Bastards.

Tiger set out to join The Bastards in a two-wheeled Cape cart drawn by six mules and carrying six persons, himself included, and their kit. The country through which they travelled was thick with Boers so they normally lay hid during the day and only moved at night, cursing the rattle of their huge, iron-clad wheels (some seven feet in diameter and at least a foot wide) against the stones. They could not carry lights as they made their way over hills and along valleys where there were often no roads. Even where there were roads they generally could not be used because the party had to make detours to avoid all inhabited places which might be occupied by the enemy.

After toiling painfully on for two weeks, the Cape cart came up with The Bastards at a place called Upington on the Orange River. In due course the commanding officer, a Colonel Birbeck, ordered Tiger, now aged nineteen and an officer of some three weeks standing, to join the garrison of Koimoes which numbered about two hundred and fifty officers and men.

'You'll have to find your own way there,' Colonel Birbeck told him. 'I haven't anyone to spare either as escort or guide.'

'That's all right, sir,' Tiger said. 'May I ask how far it is?'

'About twenty miles. Stick to the river and you can't go wrong. But you will have to keep your eyes skinned.'

'I'm used to that, sir,' Tiger replied. He did not add that he only had one.

'Well, you'll need eyes in the back of your head as well as in front,' Colonel Birbeck warned. 'The last we heard of Koimoes, there was a Boer commando hanging round the place. It was more or less surrounded.'

'Yes, sir,' Tiger said. 'When do I start?'

'I'll leave that to you,' Colonel Birbeck told him. 'You had better see the quartermaster before you go and get him to give you anything you need.'

Tiger decided to start at sunset so that he could get part of the way before it was quite dark. Before he left, he reported to Colonel Birbeck who wished him good luck, adding:

'If I don't hear from you in a couple of days, I shall assume you haven't got through.'

'Yes, sir,' Tiger said again.

All was quiet as he rode out. There were some isolated farms along the track for the first few miles; then he was in open country with the river on one side, and the broad, undulating, unfathomable veld on the other.

He let his horse have its head knowing that it was sure-footed enough not to stumble so that he could concentrate on using his two ears and his one sound eye. It was a bright night, without a moon, and the only sounds came from the horse displacing an occasional stone.

He had to estimate how far he had gone by guessing his pony's walking speed which he judged to be about four miles an hour. This meant that, barring obstacles, human or natural, he should reach Koimoes in five hours—well before midnight.

He had no intention of trying to approach the garrison while it was dark—they could not possibly know who he was. In their place, he would shoot first and answer questions afterwards.

So, when he judged he was near Koimoes, he reined in his pony and examined the lie of the land as old Lyons had taught him to do. Were there any buildings? Any camp fires or smoke? Any trees? A hollow? Or rocks?

A low, straight line caught his attention some way ahead. He found it was a wall which soon turned sharply away from the track.

'Just the place,' he said to himself. 'Out of sight of the path. And no scorpions.'

So he lay down on top of the wall, with his arm through the reins, and went to sleep.

When he woke, it was already daylight and his pony was still munching contentedly at the grass he had collected for it before going to sleep. With his arm still through the reins, he again examined his surroundings.

This time he did not need his telescope—he found he had ridden closer to Koimoes than he intended.

He had, in fact, ridden right into the place and the sentries had not seen him.

The embarrassed garrison asked him how he had managed to pass through the Boer lines. Tiger had to confess that he did not know—he only knew, but tactfully refrained from saying so, that he had got right inside the garrison's. The mystery of how he failed to meet the Boers deepened a few days later when it was learnt that the Boers had decamped on the night of Tiger's arrival and gone off to try to surprise Upington. He must have passed them on his way to Koimoes.

The South African War was the kind Tiger revelled in—a war between armed men, not machines; one in which individuals pitted their wits, strength and personal skill against each other under the stars, moon and sun.

At that time, the British forces were trying to immobilize the Boers by rounding up their horses and they offered a reward of two shillings for every live horse brought into the British lines. Every horse captured meant a serious reduction of the enemy's power to carry on with their hit and run tactics.

On one occasion, Tiger and his men stalked a Boer commando and managed to get away with six thousand horses during the night. The commando itself probably consisted of not more than five hundred men—each Boer had from five horses upwards: two to ride and the rest to carry the equipment. When the war ended, Tiger found himself in credit to the tune of more than eighteen hundred pounds. Part of it was back pay. But most of it was horse prize money.

Some weeks after Tiger went to Koimoes by night, he went back to Upington in broad daylight. Once again, he was by himself—until he saw a Boer on horseback, and incongruously

wearing a white shirt, keeping pace with him on the far side
of the Orange River.

Tiger deduced, both from his position (which was on the
skyline) and the colour of his shirt, that the Boer was a scout
who wanted his friends to see him and that the friends were
sufficiently numerous for him not to worry about his own
personal safety. But, on which side of the river were they?
The scout's or Tiger's?

He did not know for certain till he was within about a couple
of miles of Upington when he saw a cloud of dust ahead and
a friendly Boer shouted to him from the window of the farm
he was passing:

'They have just been here and stripped my farm of everything: horses, food, money—everything I have. Now they
have gone to attack Upington.'

Tiger rode cautiously on, wondering how he could circum-
vent the cloud of dust ahead of him. Then, suddenly, out of
nowhere, he saw six Boers, on horseback, crossing his path only
a couple of hundred yards ahead and making for the river.

He happened to be passing a shallow 'pan' scarcely more
than five feet deep. He slipped into it, and off his horse, as
quickly as he could without hurrying. Then he threw the reins
over a bush and looked cautiously out. He knew himself to be
a match for many more than six Boers coming at him across
open country when he was under cover.

Either the Boers had not seen him, or did not wish to, and
presently they disappeared. He waited a while in case The
Bastards in Upington opened fire on them—it would be
infuriating to be shot by one's own side. But once again nothing
happened and he reached his destination unmolested.

But his strangest adventure came when he was out scouting
by himself and realized with a shock that besides being a
hunter he was being hunted. While trying to throw his pursuers off the scent, he lost his bearings and, having no compass,
he was soon completely lost.

He wandered about the uninhabited veld for no less than
eight days finding water, and fodder enough, but nothing to
eat for himself after he had finished his iron rations.

On the eighth day, about an hour before sundown, he saw a

farm and made for it at once, past caring whether the occupant was an enemy or a friend.

The old Boer who owned the farm saw him reeling with fatigue as he rode towards it.

'God!' he said to himself in utter astonishment. 'It is as though my Piet were riding towards me—whom I laid in his grave only two weeks ago.'

As he helped Tiger tenderly off his pony, he said:

'You are welcome. You are so like my boy who is dead. Have no fear, therefore. I will take care of you.'

Then he pointed to a ring Tiger was wearing and added:

'It seems too that you are a Mason so that we are brothers.'

Tiger, being only nineteen, was not a Mason then, though he is now. The ring had belonged to an uncle who had died and his widow had given it to Tiger.

The Boer helped Tiger to a large room one side of which was deep in karosses.

'You sleep here,' the old man said, picking up a skin and folding it for Tiger to use as a pillow. 'While you take off your clothes, I will fetch you something to eat.'

Tiger sank gratefully on to the pile of skins without troubling to undress. He did not even take his spurs and boots off and he still, almost automatically, clutched his rifle to him. By the time the old man returned, he was already fast asleep, and the old Boer did not wake him.

He does not know how long he slept, but when he woke it was pitch dark. Moving his feet, he suddenly realized that there was something covering them and then that he had no boots on. Next he found that he was no longer wearing a tunic; or breeches.

His heart began to pound and his brain to work furiously. What had happened? That old man—had he betrayed him? Where was his rifle? And his revolver?

He felt for his revolver first. But his belt had gone. Then his fingers started groping for his rifle.

Instead of touching cold steel, they came in contact with something warm and soft. He stretched out his other hand. That touched something warm and soft too. What could it be?

Then a girl's voice called sleepily beside him: '*Wir kum dar*'?

She moved her leg away from his investigating fingers and sat up. So did a second girl on Tiger's other side. One of them struck a light, smiled and said to Tiger, in English:

'I will fetch you something to eat and then you must go to sleep again.'

The next morning Tiger saw that he was sharing the karosses with eighteen boys and girls of all ages between roughly six and eighteen. His neighbours seemed to be the two eldest.

They insisted on his staying with them till he got his strength back and 'muched' him like a brother while he was doing so—'Much your horses' being the word of command used in the cavalry in those days when the men dismounted after a parade. I think the old farmer would have liked to keep him there for good and not merely because of Tiger's resemblance to the son he had lost—the masonic ring also had something to do with it.

In the evenings, the whole family, and Tiger, would gather round an old harmonium and sing. One of the songs the two girls taught him, ran, in part, as follows:

> My wife's got the fever—
> I hope it won't leave her.
> I long to be single again.

When Tiger hummed the song to me, my thoughts flashed to India where I heard a nautch girl sing it in 1912 for the benefit of the European guests at a Hindu wedding. Her version ran:

> I long to be single again,
> For, when I was single
> My pockets was jingle.
> I long to be single again.

I never heard the song again till Tiger gave me his South African version almost half a century later.

In due course, Tiger took leave of his Boer friends and went back to his unit to find he had been posted 'missing'. His father and sister passed many anxious days wondering whether he was alive or dead. They still did not know when the Peace of Vereeniging was signed on 31st May 1902 and the war came to an end.

Some weeks later, Rosa was invited to accompany a friend to visit a hall in the Tottenham Court Road where a strange new invention called the bioscope was showing motion pictures of British soldiers marching in triumph through the streets of Cape Town.

It was the first time Rosa had seen the bioscope and she was vastly amused as the puppet-like human beings raced jerkily across the screen at ludicrous and impossible speeds.

Then, quite suddenly, she clutched her friend's arm.

'Look,' she screamed. 'There's Willie!'

She jumped up from her seat and shouted at the picture:

'Oh, Willie! I'm so glad to see you. Papa and I thought you were dead.'

Willie, as we already know, was very far from dead, thanks to the kind Boer family. But peace had come as a rather unpleasant shock both to him and The Bastards he was serving with. I am not quite sure where they were when the news reached them many days after the war ended. At one time they went within a few miles of Windhoek, the capital of what was then German South-West Africa. Of course, they had no business to be there—they were scores of miles over the border and Germany was not in the war. But they had heard that the Germans were supplying the Boers with rifles and ammunition from Windhoek and that was all the authority they wanted for their own breach of neutrality.

With the notification that the war was over, came an order that all captured horses, including those The Bastards were riding, were to be handed over forthwith to the Boers and that the men were to be sent in batches to railhead as soon as possible for demobilization in Cape Town.

Railhead at that moment was over three hundred miles away and how the men were to be got there without their horses was left to the ingenuity of Colonel Birbeck.

Tiger had the good fortune to be sent off with the first batch which consisted of eight officers, including one German who had volunteered for the British Army in spite of Kaiser Wilhelm's telegram of good wishes to President Kruger when the war started. The German was a sick man when the war ended and in no condition to make a journey of three hundred miles across the bare and inhospitable veld. But it would have been even worse for him to have stayed with the regiment which was camping out in the open with no medical attention available and no more food than the men could scrounge for themselves by hunting. The Boers themselves were too short of supplies to sell any.

Tiger's party set off, with their equipment and kit, in a four-wheeled 'prairie schooner' drawn by eight oxen with a maximum speed of two miles an hour. Railhead was at De Aar and, as the oxen lumbered patiently across the interminable veld, their destination seemed to recede instead of coming nearer. Fortunately it was winter so the weather was cool but as they went on, day after day, the giant wheels of the prairie schooner —eight feet in diameter—began to shrink in the dry atmosphere. The driver told them that the wheels would have to be soaked in water if they were not to disintegrate. But the party had no water to spare and could not find any, so, at Tiger's suggestion they urinated on them. It may have helped—but not much.

At last, Tiger and another officer, whose name was Jack Holt, decided to leave the prairie schooner, and most of their kit, and push on on foot to see if they could find help.

They set off at night and Tiger, happening to glance over his shoulder after a few miles, saw two green eyes flashing eerily in the darkness some fifteen yards behind them, but on the other side of the track.

He whispered to Holt to stop and the eyes stopped too. The two men then shouted to try to scare the beast away. The eyes vanished at once but when the men went forward again, they soon saw the eyes in the same position as before. When they crossed to the other side of the track, so did the eyes.

'What about a pot shot?' Holt suggested.

'Much too dark,' Tiger demurred.

The eyes followed them till they came to a farm and then vanished. The farm was the first Tiger had seen for days, a primitive place with cow-dung walls and a roof thatched with mealie stalks. They roused the owner who told them that the eyes must have belonged to a Cape Lion which is not a lion at all but a very large and ferocious wild cat, about the size of

47

a retriever. He added that they were lucky the beast had not attacked them.

Tiger and Jack Holt bargained with the farmer to send help to the prairie schooner as soon as day broke and then continued their journey on foot towards De Aar, feeling there was no point in going back to the others because, even if the farmer did not keep his promise, the prairie schooner only had to follow a well-marked track for a matter of ten miles or so to reach the farm. Tiger assumes the others ultimately got back safely, but he never heard of any of them again. And he lost all the kit he had left in the wagon.

Tiger's arrival in Cape Town was, as we already know, duly noted by the film cameras. A few days later, he was told that he had been gazetted out of the Army—not in the rank of lieutenant which he then held, but in the rank of captain. He has held a good many other temporary ranks since, including lieutenant, sub-lieutenant, flight lieutenant, trooper and provost marshal which made him a G.S.O.2. But he has always reverted to captain afterwards.

Captain Sarll was sent home on a troopship by no means in the steerage but in the lap of luxury—and almost, but not quite, in the laps of a bevy of pretty nurses, or they in his. He would not tell me whether he told them the story of the 'Officers' Remounts' but I should be very surprised if he didn't.

When Tiger got home, he discovered that, so far as London was concerned, the war was still far from over although peace had been signed at least three months previously. When his bosom friend Jack Pilcher, a dentist who lived in Gower Street, took him (in uniform) to see the fabulous new Kiralfy Exhibition at Earl's Court with its unique attraction, the Great Wheel, a band of students seized him and tried to carry him shoulder-high round the place.

Tiger managed to evade their clutches by saying loudly: 'Ow! Mind my legs! I had a bullet through them.' And Jack Pilcher added: 'At Colenso, you know.'

Whereupon the students cheered and retired leaving Tiger and Jack to spend the rest of the evening on the water chute. They ended the outing by diving into the pool at the bottom with their clothes on. Then they hailed a hansom and drove home.

Sir Howard Vincent inveigled Tiger into taking part in the victory march of the C.I.V., saying he did not want to go to it by himself. But he deliberately refrained from turning up and Tiger found himself at the head of the column with only the C.O. and the band in front of him. The crowd nearly tore him to pieces and he still does not know how he managed to reach the Guildhall with no other damage than the loss of the cock's feather from his hat.

He had not realized that the march was to be followed by a banquet until he reached the Guildhall and someone told him that they were sitting next to one another.

'Good Lord!' Tiger said. 'What's the menu?'

'Oh, the usual, I suppose,' the other replied. 'Turtle soup, I expect. Roast beef. Surrey chicken. Aylesbury duck. And all that.'

'I don't eat meat,' Tiger said shortly.

'Don't eat meat?' the other queried. 'What nonsense.'

'It isn't nonsense and I'm not going in,' Tiger declared.

'But you must,' the other maintained. 'Whatever will the Lord Mayor think if you don't?'

'He can think what he pleases,' Tiger replied. 'Good night.'

The mafficking died down after a while but not before the vegetarian Tiger had bought himself a monocle and collected a few policemen's helmets and broken up a few pro-Boer meetings in Hyde Park. By that time he was getting distinctly tired of being lionized, invited to dances, dinners, week-ends in the country.

The fact that the medical fraternity had insisted that he was not fit for active service had completely cured him of any lingering desire to be a doctor. But what else could he do?

If only there had been another war on!

Then Colonel H. C. Selous, the big-game hunter and explorer came to see Tiger's father. The story of his adventures roused Tiger from his growing lethargy. He thought of Mary Kingsley.

'That's what I'll do,' he told himself. 'I'll go out to Africa again. Central Africa.'

And he did.

4. BIG GAME

Tiger undoubtedly went out to Africa to shoot big game, like many other young men of his generation. But when he saw the wild beasts, great and small, in their native state, he could not go on with it, though he kept up the pretence of wanting to in case the African 'boys' he had engaged to guide him should desert, leaving him stranded among the primitive tribesfolk of the interior.

As the years went by, Tiger began to feel that he had let his ideals down by going out to kill wild beasts and he tried to forget about it. Indeed, if I had not discovered bits and pieces of information in his archives I doubt if he would have told me anything at all about his experiences in this part of the world. Though what I have been able to piece together is scrappy, it throws light on conditions in Central Africa at the beginning of the present century and reveals how great the changes have been in the course of the last fifty years.

In Tiger's opinion, not all the changes have necessarily been for the better. The Africans as he remembers them were ignorant by western standards and materially almost destitute. But they were happy, laughter-loving people, contented, mostly, with their poverty, their superstitions, their primitive way of life.

So far as shooting big game is concerned, Tiger's record is one to be proud of. He killed one elephant which somebody else had wounded and which was a real danger to the African villagers. The only lion he shot was one which clawed a piece out of his arm when he was trying to release it from a native trap. He also shot a number of antelopes to feed his African guides and porters.

His father's friend, Colonel Selous, records in his book *A Hunter's Wanderings in Africa*, that in the course of four years he shot twenty elephants, twelve rhinos, four hippopotami, eighteen giraffes, a hundred buffaloes, forty-eight zebras, seventeen warthogs, thirteen lions, three ostriches and several hundred antelopes of various species. Once, near the Zambesi, he and his partner, George Wood, killed six elephants in a single day.

The few bits and pieces I have been able to prize out of Tiger himself and from some articles on his adventures which appeared in the *People's Journal* of Dundee in February and March 1914, indicate that he went out through the Suez Canal to Mombasa and then on to Nairobi by train. The railway from the coast had only just been finished and Kenya was still known as British East Africa.

Tiger remembers Nairobi as a shell of a place with buildings which were chiefly huts and the one road a mere track. Lions prowled round it and the country outside was an endless and largely unknown vista of wilderness dotted with occasional, semi-nomadic African villages and filled with vast herds of wild animals: giraffes, zebras, buffaloes, hippopotami, rhinoceroses, antelopes of many kinds and, of course, lions.

Somewhere, Tiger engaged some 'boys', one of whom spoke a little English and was named June. As a one-man expedition, Tiger had no fixed itinerary but simply mooched around where his fancy dictated. He seems to have gone into the Belgian Congo for, in the *People's Journal* of 28th March 1914, he speaks of having come across a tribe of 'little people' who were evidently pygmies.

Seeing a small hut which did not appear to be inhabited, he stooped down to see what was in it. Meeting an intolerable stench, he lifted his head quickly. The thatch came up too and, when he had got rid of it, he saw that the hut contained a sackful of human eyes.

The next district he visited was a place called Nawalia in the Muchinga Mountains of Northern Rhodesia where the hills range up to over five thousand feet, the grass is thick and matted and dotted with trees where, in those days, elephants abounded besides other game, including lions. It was here, in fact, that Tiger made both his 'kills'.

Nawalia was then the *Boma*, or district headquarters. But when the Africans had cropped the soil till it had lost all its humus, they moved away and Nawalia disappeared without trace. Even the river, which Tiger says was called Mangus, can no longer be identified because the Africans who gave it that name have moved elsewhere and their successors call it something quite different.

When Tiger shot his lion, the 'boy' June cupped his hands to catch the blood which was flowing from Tiger's arm. Then he smeared it over his face and rubbed it into his hair, saying to Tiger:

'You mighty hunter. Me rub blood on head, me mighty hunter same like you.'

June's favourite delicacies were wheyless sour milk which had almost turned to stone and the black, oily scrapings from Tiger's pipe which he moulded in his hands and then chewed, smacking his lips and rolling his eyes in ecstasy.

News of the wounded elephant was brought to Tiger by the Africans who lived in N'Dombos, a village which has also ceased to exist. He followed the poor beast's spoor along the Mangus river among a tangle of mataity reeds with spikes as sharp as razors. Mosquitoes swarmed round him but, like the lice in the South African War, they left him severely alone.

After a while, he came to grass so thick and matted that he could scarcely fight through it. The grass teemed with snakes, mostly puff adders, but these again did not worry Tiger who, on the advice of Colonel Selous, wore stout top boots and thick, loose cord breeches. He also had a coat over his shirt but he did not wear a hat in spite of being in the tropics.

When I commented on his choice of clothing, he replied:

'What earthly sense is there in just wearing a thin pair of drawers over bare legs when you're walking through reeds like razors or grass full of poisonous snakes? A bare skin is all right when you are resting in camp but not when you're on the move. Besides, thick clothes help to keep you cool.'

After a time, Tiger heard a strange, gurgling noise ahead of him. His local tracker made signs to explain that it came from the elephants' stomachs. Next he heard a snapping, swishing sound as the elephants pulled down branches with their trunks and tore off the tender shoots to the accompaniment of frequent little squeals from the females who seemed to be talking to one another all the time.

The wounded elephant was a little apart from the herd and it took Tiger some time to get within range because the herd was constantly on the move and if any of the beasts had got wind of him they would all have stampeded, the wounded bull included. It took him several hours to reach a suitable position. Then, almost to his surprise, he saw the huge beast only some fifty yards ahead. It was standing almost broadside on with its head among the branches of a small clump of trees and its legs completely hidden in the long grass.

Tiger fired once at the brain and once at the heart. The elephant fell to its knees and then over on its side while the rest of the herd fled in all directions screaming and trumpeting with rage and fright.

Tiger immediately sent a messenger to June with instructions to strike camp immediately and come to where the dead elephant lay. The camp was a good six miles away but he need not have bothered. In less than half an hour, grinning Africans began to arrive, armed with huge baskets and long knives apparently fashioned out of iron hay-hoops. And, not long afterwards, June and the camp appeared. They had not seen the messenger who had gone by another route.

At first Tiger thought that the news must have been spread by the 'bush telegraph' Mary Kingsley had told him about. But when he asked June why he had struck camp before the messenger reached it, the 'boy' grinned and pointed to the sky.

It was black with wheeling vultures.

The villagers of N'Dombos were afraid to start cutting up the elephant's carcass until their chief gave them permission. He happened to be on a journey and it was two days before he returned. Meanwhile, the inhabitants of another village had come, with their chief, and Tiger had some difficulty in keeping the peace. His decision was to the effect that N'Dombos was entitled to the first spoils because it had provided the trackers. This was accepted without question immediately.

Two days in the hot, tropical sun made the elephant's body swell to the size of a balloon and when the word was given to start cutting, the foul gas came rushing out with a noise like a steam safety valve. A stream of filthy, dark-coloured, evil-smelling liquid followed and caught Tiger, among others, full in the face. The others seemed to enjoy it. At any rate, they roared with laughter.

Having disembowelled the carcass with their hay-hoop knives which needed sharpening every two or three minutes, the villagers leapt inside and smeared themselves from head to foot with the clotted blood which they allowed to dry on their near-naked bodies. June told Tiger this was to make them brave in battle and to protect them from evil spirits. Meanwhile, the women, most of whom had babies strapped on their backs with a kind of shawl, were tearing the elephant's flesh and entrails to pieces with their hands and stuffing it into the baskets.

Suddenly the laughter and chatter which punctuated the chaos was interrupted by loud screams and Tiger saw three women all tugging at the same long, disgusting piece of entrail. While the women tugged and cursed one another with shrill screams of invective, the men formed a circle round them and cheered them on.

The fun lasted till one of the men slashed unexpectedly at the coveted piece with his knife with the result that all three women fell flat on their backs and the men laughed louder than ever.

During the four days that followed, the villagers gorged themselves to a state of intoxication which they increased by smoking large quantities of hemp. They were unable to do any kind of work for a week.

After Tiger shot the elephant, he found that his fame as a hunter went before him and, every time he moved, his camp was surrounded by whole villages all anxious to guide him, without payment, to the places where wild beasts were plentiful. When they found that Tiger would not shoot to provide them with free meals the local Africans left him one by one. June told him they had come to the conclusion that 'big fellow no much hunter. No good for *M'futa*.'

M'futa meant fat.

In due course, Tiger went back to London with his one pair of tusks which weighed between them ninety-one and a half pounds. He estimated that they would fetch at least £200 but when they were sold on the Ivory Floor of St. Katherine's

Dock, where African ivory is still sold every Tuesday, the predecessor of the present superintendent, Mr. Yates, pronounced them to be defective and all Tiger got was £70.

He spent the money—and a good deal more—on fitting himself out to go to Canada.

5. ACROSS CANADA

TIGER's experiences in Canada would alone fill a book. He went there soon after the turn of the century when most of the country was still as little known as the parts of Africa he had just left. Its vast breadth had been spanned by railways; there was thought to be untold gold in the Klondyke if a man had the guts to go and dig it out; there were forests to be felled if you could stand a temperature of many degrees below zero; there were farms where brawn was essential. And that, so far as Great Britain was concerned, was Canada.

Which, of course, was why Tiger decided to go there.

Two friends went with him, Harcourt Emra and Gray. That is to say, they all three travelled on the same boat, the *Heron*—Emra and Gray as passengers and Tiger as a deck hand. He said he wanted to toughen his muscles for the Canadian way of life, but I think he also wanted to see what regular work on the ocean wave was really like. And he was hard up.

The *Heron* appears to have been an ugly-looking tramp but a surprisingly good seaboat. It took her the best part of a fortnight to cross the Atlantic but this was partly because, when she neared the mouth of the St. Lawrence, she had to thread her way excitingly through hundreds of flashing, jewelled icebergs towering high into the air above the pygmy ship.

After steaming interminably between the distant, wooded banks of the great river, the *Heron* reached Quebec where Tiger heard reveille being sounded on a Japanese cruiser which lay at anchor dressed over-all from stem to stern via both deck and mastheads with the sailors' washing, so that she looked more like a floating laundry than a warship.

Tiger and his two friends went ashore and duly made a pilgrimage to the Heights of Abraham where Wolfe and Montcalm battled to decide whether Canada should adorn the French Crown or the British. Then they went on to Montreal which seemed to them to consist wholly of hideous grain elevators.

Gray petered out in Montreal and Tiger never heard of him again. He himself went with Harcourt Emra to Ottawa where

Emra was bitten with the idea of buying a farm, though he knew nothing whatsoever about farming. Tiger could not afford to join his friend's venture and they agreed that he should hire himself out as a farm-hand first so as to learn the ropes. By the time he had done so, he had had enough of farming and Emra had lost so much money that he had descended to the farm-hand level; so the partnership never materialized.

Tiger's first employer was a man named Sparrow who made Tiger sleep in an outhouse in case he should corrupt the morals of Miss Sparrow, a female whom Tiger remembers as a scraggy, pimply, breastless, unwashed broomstick of about twenty-five only slightly less unattractive than her father who went around with a Bible in one hand and his cash-box in the other.

Sparrow expected Tiger to get up at five a.m. and work until it was dark. He did not provide a bed, only straw. The broomstick put Tiger's meals out for him on the step outside the kitchen. Where he ate them was his affair but he was supposed to wash the plate under the pump before he put it back where he had found it. He was not allowed a candle in case he should set the straw on fire. He was not supposed to smoke but I have no doubt he did. Sparrow offered him five dollars a month and his keep. Tiger insisted on ten and Sparrow agreed to pay but he did not pay a cent.

Tiger learnt his job, and bided his time, for nearly three months without complaining. Then, one day, Sparrow happened to come on him just sitting and doing nothing else—he had finished his lunch in less than half an hour and reckoned he still had half an hour's free time due to him.

Sparrow thought otherwise and danced up to him with heckles bristling.

'Didn' I tell you I won' hev no loafin'?' he began. 'Ye've had yr dinner. Now git down to it. Didn' I tell you th't when you've nuthen else, you goes an' digs that 'tater patch? Well, go an' dig it.'

'I'm entitled to an hour's rest at noon,' Tiger said without moving.

'You ain't entitled to no sich thing,' Sparrow yelled. 'No, sirree.'

'Oh, I'm not, aren't I?' Tiger said, getting up and walking over to the potato patch. He drove the fork in so hard that it sank to the haft. Then he turned to Sparrow and said:

'There's your fork and there are your potatoes. Dig them yourself. I'm going.'

He added:

'I've slept like a dog and eaten like a hog: beans as salt as hell. Beans. Beans. Nothing but beans. And so far you haven't paid me a cent. If you were a man, I'd give you the biggest hiding any man ever had. But you're too filthy to soil my hands on. If you don't get out of my sight this minute, I'll hold you under the pump and scrub the hide off you. It'd be the first real wash you've had since I've been here.'

He advanced menacingly towards Sparrow who evidently thought he intended to carry out his threat for he ran for his life into the house. Tiger packed his bag, hoisted it on to his shoulder and started to walk away. He was too disgusted even to go and demand his money.

As he was opening the gate, Sparrow rushed after him and said:

'Wait a minute. What'll folks think? I'll give you thirty-five dollars a months ef you'll stay. My daughter says yer worth it. See, here's the three months' money I owe you. An' here's a present to show I ain't harbourin' no ill feelings.'

He had been counting out thirty dollars as he spoke and he now ostentatiously added another sixty.

Tiger took the roll of notes and counted out twenty dollars—the third month was not quite finished so he did not feel entitled to more. Then he threw the rest of the money at Sparrow's feet and walked away without a word.

He spent his twenty dollars, and the next three or four days, eating and sleeping at the village inn after which he took a job with another farmer who offered without being asked five more dollars a month than Sparrow had steeled himself to promise. His new employer also gave him a decent room, a proper bed and first-class food.

Even so, Tiger again only stayed three months.

He says he moved because he could not get any good books in the village nor strings for his banjo. Obviously, the true reason was that he was bored stiff with the monotony of being perpetually in the same place, pushing a fork, or a spade, endlessly into unresponsive, unresisting soil and turning the sods over one by one, day after day, week after week.

Nearly sixty years after, I have found it impossible to sort out the order of the various steps Tiger took next to get the itch out of his restless feet. He certainly tried his hand as a teamster in a Canadian forestry concern in Northern Ontario. It was there that he had his first sight of a full-grown bull moose. He had noticed a hard, narrow track which crossed the soft, virgin snow and he followed it to see if he could find out what made it. Then, suddenly, he was standing close to the moose using the track on its way from its lair to its feeding-ground. It was a magnificent beast with a huge spread of antlers—a majestic, solitary, harmless creature larger, but more helpless, than the lions of Africa. He left it with a feeling of awe and pity.

On another day he saw two brown bears playing with one another among the trees. They did not know he was there and they obviously enjoyed gambolling in the snow just as much as Tiger did.

Tiger also drove a team for some months in Wyoming. But what he remembers most vividly is a visit to Dawson City in the fabulous Yukon.

It must have been in 1903 or 1904 that he went there in company with two men whose names he has forgotten. It was already late in the season and very cold as they toiled over the White Horse Pass carrying a tent and their supplies on their backs. It took them all their strength to get to Dawson City. The miners they found there were a suspicious, hot-tempered lot, quick on the draw and not pleased to see new faces. The glamour of the famous Klondyke gold rush at the end of the nineteenth century had already faded and gold had become hard to find. So the miners who were already established regarded all newcomers much as a trade unionist regards a black-leg. When Tiger told them he had simply come to look round and go away again, they thought he was lying. Some of them said so.

Tiger found Dawson City an impoverished, down-at-heel little place consisting of a single very dirty street of little wooden shacks with corrugated iron roofs and verandas with hitching posts for horses. Many of the shacks were saloons but there were only two barmaids who alternated between serving drinks and dancing the cancan.

Having seen all they wanted of Dawson City, Tiger and his two companions bought a canoe from an Indian they met at the wooden jetty on the Yukon river. It was a lovely, fragile thing—just a few ribs of wood covered with birch bark scarcely thicker than a sheet of parchment. Yet it carried the three of them with ease, and their gear, together with a stone weighing over a hundredweight which was fixed in the bows. It cost a pound of plug tobacco for which they had paid a dollar—five shillings in those days.

They hesitated a long while before buying the canoe. A journey of a thousand miles lay before them along a river which they knew to be full of rapids, rocks, whirlpools and other dangers. How could such a fragile thing possibly negotiate such hazards; especially when the canoeists were novices?

The owner of the canoe laughed at them. He was a strange-looking individual with tobacco-darkened teeth and he looked more like an Eskimo than an Indian. He only had a few words of English and he mimed what he could not speak.

'Keep her straight,' he told them. 'Don't try to avoid the rocks. The canoe will do that on its own. Where the water is too shallow, get out and carry her.'

After he had taken them out and shown them, they saw what he meant, and as they journeyed on down the Yukon they found he was absolutely right.

The backwash set up when the water dashed itself against a rock pushed the canoe's nose away just as it seemed that it was hurtling to inevitable destruction. And when the pliant birch bark did graze against a rock, it simply bent instead of splitting.

The three adventurers started their thousand-mile trip by dipping their paddles first on one side and then on the other, because each stroke slewed the canoe's nose round. As they passed an Indian, he shouted at them and made graphic signs to show them where they would soon find themselves unless they paddled correctly.

'You want me teach?' he asked, paddling alongside.

First he wanted five sticks of plug tobacco for the lesson but he finally accepted three. Showing them how to keep the canoe on course by a flick of the wrist at the end of each stroke took him about a minute but the lesson was cheap at the price.

After that, the only time the three novices came really near disaster was on the morning after they left Dawson City.

'I can't see what we want that blasted stone for,' Tiger remarked. 'I'm sure we would go much faster if we threw it overboard.'

The other two agreed, so he went forward, unshipped the stone and toppled it into the water.

As he came back to his seat amidship, the canoe raised its nose into the air and the Yukon began to pour into the stern. They only just got to shore before the canoe sank.

When they had lifted her out and emptied the water out of her, they started to look for another stone. It took them almost the whole day to find one.

They could only travel during the daytime and camped on shore each night. At some point they crossed the Canadian border into Alaska and in due course arrived at another shack town called Circle. Hearing shots just before they reached it, they beached their canoe and hurried to see who had fired them. Presently they found a man lying unconscious on the ground bleeding profusely—a bullet had gone right through his leg. Tiger bandaged him as best he could and then the three of them carried him to the canoe. He was immensely tall, nearly seven feet, but as thin as a lath.

Tiger, looking at the unconscious giant's hands, decided that he was an educated man. When he was able to speak, he told Tiger that he was a Belgian named Paul J. Selles. He spoke English almost perfectly with a marked American accent which soon began to wear off as he and Tiger talked together.

Paul Selles, like Tiger, had gone to the Yukon out of curiosity. The guides he had engaged to show him round had picked a quarrel with him, shot him and decamped with everything they found in his pockets and kit. But they overlooked the leather belt full of gold sovereigns which he wore next to his skin—much to Tiger's relief. He would have found it difficult

61

to supply even the single penny which the Good Samaritan provided for the man who fell among thieves on the equally desolate but much warmer road between Jerusalem and Jericho.

Although the two men had much in common, Tiger could not wait in Circle to team up with Paul when the Belgian recovered. The obvious reason was financial; but there was another: the Russo-Japanese War had started, and Tiger was itching to join in.

So he hurried on down the Yukon and once there, of course, nothing could stop him from making his way to Manchuria.

Japan was Britain's ally in those days, so we can assume that Tiger did not offer his services to the Russians. If he offered them to the Japanese, they certainly did not let him fight, which may account for the gaps in his memory. He never forgets a fight.

He does, however, remember seeing Japanese soldiers in training and marvelling at the way their minds worked. Some two hundred and fifty of them were trying to turn themselves into cavalry, but they scarcely knew which way round to sit on their horses.

Then, one day, he saw them drilling with ladders. There was no wall to lean them against and the ladders were at least twelve feet long. At the word of command, each little Japanese soldier ran to the top and balanced himself there while he fired his rifle at a distant target, after which he ran down to earth again. The whole exercise impressed Tiger greatly, and the number of hits simply amazed him.

The role of interested spectator, however, does not appeal to Tiger and we very soon find him back in Canada as handyman for a farmer named White in Ontario. White himself was far gone with tuberculosis and worked as though each day was to be his last. It was winter, and in the long evenings after work was over, White and Tiger used to sit in front of the fire arguing—mostly about philosophy on which Tiger still holds views which stem from his early meeting with Annie Besant.

White had five pretty daughters and when they could bear the battle of words no longer, they bore down on the monocled handyman and carried him off to play Postman's Knock,

Hunt the Slipper, Blind Man's Buff and Kiss in the Ring. There is no reason to suppose that Tiger, who was now twenty-two or twenty-three, would have preferred to go on talking philosophy.

About midnight, there would often be a jingle of sleigh bells outside. Then the White girls and Tiger would rush to the doors. Another moment and some twenty or thirty other youngsters were inside and a corner of the room was littered higgledy-piggledy with furs which today would fetch many thousands of pounds. By this time, Tiger would have pulled out his banjo and somebody else a fiddle. The chairs and table were pushed to one side and everybody was dancing. When they tired of dancing, someone (and it could have been Tiger) suggested a game of Kiss in the Ring.

On other nights, the White girls and Tiger would jump into a sleigh, round up some neighbours and dash off to a farm maybe ten miles away, arriving without warning or premeditation and sure of a welcome. The housewife never minded: the self-invited guests brought their food with them. All she had to do was provide something to drink. It might be cider, or even applejack, but much more often it was just tea or coffee.

Tiger's memory of these harmless junketings is still green after more than half a century. But the description I like best is one written thirty years ago which I found among his papers.

'There used to be dozens of sleighs [he wrote]. All the people in them were covered with furs and in the bottom of the sleighs were heaps of straw or heated stones to keep everyone snug.

'How wonderful it was! The bright moonlight! The white snow, the jingle of the sleigh bells, the jolly, laughing faces of the lads and lasses, the peals of merry laughter awakening the echoes of the night as we dash along at a smart pace, the horses pulling well. On we glide, up hill and down dale, through avenues of wonderful pine trees, hung with fairy crystals sparkling like diamonds in the clear moonlight. . . . My moustache is as hard as a piece of stone. I could, if I liked, break it off like glass.

'What a wonderful feeling of exhilaration I have as I stand

63

up in the front of the big bobsleigh, holding the reins, with my feet firmly planted and my body braced back as we fly over the crest of a hill and commence a downward rush. We have no brakes. All depends on the sharp-shod horses and the skill of the driver. . . .'

And, half an hour earlier, the youngsters had had no idea they were going to leave their firesides. Maybe the telephone, which practically insists that everything should be planned in advance, is not such a happy invention after all.

But there was plenty of work to be done too at White's farm, even in winter. White was short of water, so Tiger and a carpenter he used to call Jack spent interminable hours driving six-foot lengths of iron piping down through the kitchen floor. The 'mallet' was a huge, iron-clad piece of wood with a hole from side to side through which ran an iron bar for use as a handle. This contraption weighed at least one and a half hundredweight and each time Tiger and Jack let it fall it drove the pipe down one inch.

The first section of piping was pointed and had holes in it with a filter arrangement in front to prevent the holes becoming clogged as the pipe was driven through the earth. When the first section was within two or three inches of the floor, Jack screwed in another and so it went on, lift, drop, hour after hour, day after day, an inch at a time. It was a good thing there were other chores to do—feeding the livestock, cutting and carrying logs for the fires, sweeping away the frequent fresh falls of snow. Otherwise, the monotony of pipe-driving would have been unbearable.

Tiger and Jack struck water at the nine hundredth inch—at seventy-five feet. They were lucky. A neighbour (for whom Harcourt Emra had gone to work after the failure of his farm venture) struck rock, not water, at three hundred feet. He and Emra made no less than four more equally deep boreholes before finding water.

White had a hot temper and he and Tiger quarrelled so violently one evening over nothing in particular that Tiger left the following morning in spite of floods of tears from the White girls and, I think, a few from himself. He went straight to Ottawa where he had left a suitcase, changed into his evening

clothes for the first time in more than a year and took himself,
by himself, to the theatre.

The play was *Tess of the d'Urbervilles* and it made him feel so
miserable that he left at the end of the second act.

From Ottawa he went to Toronto where he regained his
spirits by racing over the frozen waters of Lake Ontario in an
ice yacht at eighty m.p.h. It was his first experience of this
sport and he capsized on to the ice more times than he can
remember. By the time he had more or less got the knack of
it he had run through most of the money he had earned, and
been unable to spend, at the Whites.

He had had quite enough of farming—for the moment at
any rate. But he could not think of anything better to do till
someone happened to mention the Royal Canadian Dragoons.

'Really, you know,' he remarked. 'That's a jolly good idea.
I think I'll have a bash at it.'

6. ROYAL CANADIAN DRAGOONS

So Tiger packed most of his belongings into a bag which he stored in the town, hailed a sleigh and told the driver to take him to Stanley Barracks which the Royal Canadian Dragoons shared with the Royal Canadian Infantry. It was the devil's own day, with a gale of wind and driving snow. At the end of Spadina Avenue, the driver turned his horse too quickly and the sleigh capsized, tipping Tiger head first into six feet of snow. The driver managed to drag him out before he was suffocated but the haversack in which he was carrying his razor and etceteras was lost without trace.

'Sorry about it,' the driver said. 'Never known me horse do a damn' fool thing like that before.'

'That's all right,' Tiger replied. 'What's the fare?'

The driver said it was one dollar fifty cents.

'Can you change a ten-dollar bill?' Tiger inquired. 'I'm afraid I have nothing smaller.'

The driver couldn't. The barrack gate was only just across the road so Tiger suggested their going together to see if the guard could change the note.

'I've come to enlist,' Tiger explained to the N.C.O. in charge, Sergeant Doré. 'The driver who brought me can't change a ten-dollar bill. I wonder if you can help us?'

Sergeant Doré counted out the one dollar fifty cents without speaking and the driver left.

'Thank you very much, Sergeant,' Tiger said, taking out his wallet.

There was nothing in it.

Tiger searched his pockets—each pocket several times. He still found nothing. Not even a cent. Yet he was absolutely certain he had left the hotel with one bill for one hundred dollars, one for twenty dollars and three for ten dollars. Had the driver taken them when he was dragging Tiger out of the snow? It was possible, of course, but if so, why hadn't he taken the whole wallet?

A year or so later, when Tiger left the R.C.D., he found the notes tucked away in an inside pocket of the civilian waistcoat he was wearing when he went to Stanley Barracks.

But, at the time, Sergeant Doré took a very poor view indeed of the matter. However, when Tiger promised faithfully to pay him back when he received his pay, he agreed to take no action at the moment.

The Commanding Officer, Colonel Lessard, who was a French Canadian, looked Tiger up and down, eyeglass and all, asked a few questions about the Boer War, and finally sent him to the medical officer who looked first at Tiger's eye and said:

'My good man, it's no earthly use your coming to see me with an eye like that. It's obvious you can't shoot.'

Tiger, who had heard the same thing twice before, replied:

'But, sir, I was the crack marksman in my old regiment. And my blind eye made no difference to my shooting during the Boer War.'

'If I say you can't shoot, you can't shoot,' the doctor told him, 'so don't argue. You're here for me to examine you, not to shoot your mouth.'

'Yes, sir,' Tiger said, clicking his heels together. And in the end the doctor passed him.

For the next few weeks, Tiger's name was 'on the gate', which meant that he was on probation and not entitled to an issue of walking-out kit so that he was, in effect, confined to barracks.

At first he hated it, especially as he hadn't a cent. Then an entirely unexpected windfall arrived in the shape of fifty pounds back pay due to him from his South African war service. It had been chasing him round Canada for months. He immediately paid his debt to Sergeant Doré and then stood everybody drinks in the canteen. After that he felt quite happy—in two senses.

Tiger considers that he owes his present capacity to absorb beer mainly to his training at Stanley Barracks. The men had a 'birthday party' every night. Tiger played the mandolin and another man the saxophone. There was one chap who always got drunk and insisted on drooling out 'I'm a man wot's done wrong to me parents'. At the end of the last verse, he used to burst from song into tears. This was the signal for crusts of bread to be thrown at him and beer mugs to be emptied over him after which he was crowned with an inverted spittoon—one which had been in constant use throughout the evening.

When Tiger went to Stanley Barracks, he could cope with about ten pints at a session and he was greatly concerned to find that his more seasoned boon companions could outdrink him by fifteen pints and even more. He soon learnt to catch them up. Some fifty years later, to be exact on Armistice Day, 1959, he came back to my house as sober as any judge after downing thirty pints between midday and 11 p.m.

He thoroughly disapproves of drunkenness. His view is that if a man cannot hold his liquor, he should not drink.

Discipline in the R.C.D. was strict on parade. At other times the men could do pretty well what they liked. There were fights every Saturday evening in the Riding School when scores were paid off. There were practical jokes and wild horseplay at any time.

One of the most hated men in the regiment was the Orderly Room Sergeant's deputy, known to one and all as 'Flannel Feet' because he used to tie a piece of sacking round his boots to help him pry into other folks' business.

The night after Tiger's arrival, Flannel Feet started to haze a man so unmercifully that the victim finally gave him a crack on the jaw and ended up in the guardroom. The barrack-room lads were extremely angry and the following night, after Lights Out, first one and then another crept out of bed and urinated into Flannel Feet's top boots which were standing invitingly by his bedside ready for him to pull on when reveille sounded the next morning.

The trick paid off handsomely. Flannel Feet leapt out of bed when the trumpeter started to blow, thrust both feet simultaneously into his boots and was rewarded by a squelch of liquid squirting up all over him, even into his face.

Flannel Feet himself was late on parade that morning but everybody else was out of the room in record time, including Tiger who was almost doubled up with laughter.

Tiger's name soon came 'off the gate', for there was very little even Canadians could teach him about riding. They found he could shoot, too. In fact, they chose him to lead the left file in the Long Distance Marching and Firing Competition for the championship of the Canadian Army.

The R.C.D.'s rivals were their neighbours, the R.C.I., who naturally fancied their chances of marching ten miles on foot in full kit with rifle and ammunition against a team accustomed to move on horseback.

But the R.C.D. team completed the marching test at a good six m.p.h., arriving at the shooting range fifteen minutes before their opponents who only had two minutes to spare before they were due at the butts. The targets were the usual disappearing 'men' who came up for ten seconds and then popped down again.

The R.C.D. scored with every shot. Their opponents did not. Their hands were still too shaky.

One day, a new recruit arrived who, at six feet eight inches, was a good four inches taller than Tiger. He was a cadaverous, loose-limbed chap with a hooked nose and reminded Tiger irresistibly of Don Quixote at first. He was an American who soon became known as Montana Jim.

Montana's thirst was on a par with Tiger's and, as they put the pints away, the American put his arm round Tiger's shoulder and said:

'Ah dessay you're a-wonderin' what's brought an Amurrican ter jine a racket like this. Well, pal, ah'll tell you. But you mus' prawmiss me first you won't tell on me. Boy, ah don' wan' no trouble but ah guess ah can trus' you ef you prawmiss.'

Tiger promised and Montana went on in a confidential whisper:

'Well, pal, et's like this heear. Ah'm from Montanna. Ah gotter ranch there. Bigger'n all hell. Yes, sirree. An' the beautifullest wife you ever saw. Real dandy. . . .'

He lifted his glass and drained it silently, but obviously in her honour.

'Yes, sirree,' he went on after Tiger had taken appropriate action in regard to the empty glass. 'A reel peach, she is. Name of Mirandy. About up ter ma armpit. . . .'

'Any children?' Tiger queried.

'We ain't ben married that along,' Montana confessed. 'But there will be. Ah'll see to that. Where wuz I? Ah yes. Well, a man an' me, we had a bit of an argyment. Ah didn' like the way he looked at ma wife an' nor did she. We'd both had a spot of rye an' he came up agin ma fist. When they went ter pick him up, he were dead. So ah had to beat it across the border into Canady. Janie said she'd write an' tell me when it's blown over. Say, boy, do ah wish she'd write!'

'I thought you said her name was Miranda,' Tiger remarked.

'Thass right,' Montana agreed. 'Mirandy. But ah call her Janie. More friendly like. . . . Say, you wouldn' hev ten bucks you c'd lend a feller so ah c'n send her a present? Ah ain't got as much as a dime.'

Tiger lent him ten dollars. A day or two later, he also lent Montana his kit issue knife, fork and spoon (bearing Tiger's regimental number, 2204) because Montana said he had lost his and did not want to be deficient at kit inspection.

The letter Montana was expecting from Miranda Jane arrived not long afterwards and contained a passage which he showed to Tiger saying that the affair had now blown over so she hoped her husband would come home as soon as possible.

'An' that,' Montana said, 'is what ah'd sure like ter do. But how'm ah gwine ter do it when ah need twen'y-five bucks f'r ma purchase money an' another fifty ter get ma clothes aht of pawn. Say, pal, you wouldn't be able ter help a pal, would you?'

Tiger has always been willing to accommodate a pal, but he has not always been able. On this occasion he was both. So, the following afternoon, Montana went down town ostensibly to redeem his civilian clothes before buying himself out of the regiment.

He was carried back to barracks the same evening, fighting drunk and without either his civilian clothes or a cent.

Tiger presumably told Montana exactly what he thought of him and he was grooming his horse on the morning after he had done so when Montana strolled over, lashed out at Tiger's jaw without saying a word and sent him sprawling. As Tiger was picking himself up, Montana knocked him down again.

This time Tiger decided to stay down and after a few moments Montana laughed contemptuously and walked away.

When he had gone, Tiger got up, felt his jaw rather gingerly and, finding it still in one piece, went on with his grooming, acutely conscious that some of his comrades were jeering at him for having let Montana hit him without even trying to hit back.

'So they think I'm a coward, do they?' Tiger said to himself. 'Well, let's see.'

Having finished his grooming, Tiger went to Montana's barrack room where he saw the American standing on his bed. He had Tiger's mess knife in one hand and the fork in the other and he waved them derisively in their owner's face as Tiger came up to him.

'All right, you low-down skunk,' Tiger said, 'we both know they're mine. Are you going to hand them over peaceably? Or must I take them? I need them for kit inspection tomorrow, as you damn' well know.'

'Come an' take 'em, Limey bastard,' Montana jeered, leaning forward.

Tiger flashed out with his left and Montana quickly brought up his right arm to ward off the blow. Then, to Tiger's immense surprise, Montana's knees gave way and he collapsed on to the bed.

Before Tiger's one good eye had been able to take in what had happened, he found himself surrounded by an angry, milling crowd of Montana's room-mates who knocked him down, hauled him to his feet, twisted his arms behind his back and frog-marched him to the lake where they tossed him into the water and threw stones at him when he started to swim to the landing stage.

Realizing that they would not let him land, Tiger swam away, his head reeling not only from the blows he had received but with astonishment at the way he had been treated. Surely he had every right to give Montana a clip on the jaw when the swine would not return the borrowed mess kit? Besides, Montana had hit him first. So why had he been almost lynched?

He did not find out until he had dragged himself out of the water, well out of sight of his comrades, and returned, wet, cold, bruised and indignant, to Stanley Barracks. When he reached the gate, he was immediately put under close arrest and marched off to the cells.

'But what am I supposed to have done?' he protested.

'Killed a comrade by stabbing him with a fork,' Sergeant Doré told him. 'Your fork. With your regimental number on it.'

'Nonsense,' Tiger replied. 'I didn't do anything of the kind. The swine borrowed my mess knife, fork and spoon and I went to ask him to give them back for tomorrow's kit inspection. He refused, so I hit him with my fist. He actually had my things in his hand at the time.'

'Oh yeah?' Sergeant Doré remarked. 'Then, how do you account for the fact that your fork—your fork, mind you—was sticking in the poor devil's neck? So deep it took six men to hold him while it was pulled out.'

'I told you,' Tiger repeated. 'He had my fork in his hand when I hit out at him. I suppose my fist must have struck his forearm instead of his jaw and driven the fork back against his neck. Anyway, I swear I wasn't holding the damn' thing. And everybody in my barrack room knows he borrowed my eating irons.'

'You've got a lively imagination, I must say,' Sergeant Doré remarked, obviously unconvinced. 'And that poor devil can't contradict you, being dead.'

Fortunately, he was not dead and, in due course, he recovered. Meanwhile, Tiger's friends in his own barrack room were able to testify that Montana had indeed borrowed the fork with which he had been wounded and that Tiger had gone to get it back. And, in the end, Montana himself admitted that he was holding the fork when Tiger hit him.

But the feud smouldered on and finally Tiger challenged Montana to fight it out in the Riding School.

When Saturday night arrived, the Riding School was packed. The betting slightly favoured Montana who had the longer reach and two eyes to Tiger's one. If the men had realized that Tiger's one good eye was only half an eye without its eyeglass, the odds against him would no doubt have been much longer. But the audience, and more important, his opponent, undoubtedly thought of the eyeglass as affectation and gave Tiger credit for at least one sound eye, possibly two.

There were no seconds in the Riding School affrays, no gloves and no ring except a ring of excited spectators, milling, yelling and gesticulating in the saw-dusted, and often bloody, arena. Nor were there any rounds. Once battle was joined it went on until one or other of the combatants was down for good.

Montana went for Tiger's face and had him on the floor no less than three times in the first few minutes. Tiger left Montana's face alone and concentrated on his body, especially his stomach. His own left eye was soon closed but he did not mind—he could not see out of it anyway. His nose was bleeding too but he went doggedly on, not trying to guard but raining blow after blow against Montana's lower ribs and where he judged his diaphragm was.

After about ten minutes, Montana's fists had lost their sting and, after fifteen, they felt like doughnuts when they touched Tiger's face. And Montana's breathing sounded like an engine steaming out of a station. Soon afterwards, he sank to the ground and stayed there, whereupon Tiger's backers yelled obscene endearments at him and carried him to his quarters in triumph.

A few days passed and then, one morning, Montana was reported missing. He never came back. It was soon found that Tiger was not the only person to whom he owed money. Sergeant Skinner, for example, was the poorer by one hundred dollars and a revolver. Tiger himself lost not only the money Montana had borrowed but also his Boer War medals. And the thief was never caught.

Almost exactly thirty years later, Tiger received a letter from the War Office in London. It was dated 16th January 1935 and had the honour to inform him that his 'Queen's South Africa Medal with clasps "Tugela Heights", and "The Relief of Ladysmith" and "Cape Colony" and the King's South Africa Medal with clasps "South Africa, 1901" and "South Africa, 1902" had been found in Canada and returned to the War Office by the Canadian Military authorities.'

The letter concluded by asking Captain Sarll what he would like done with them.

Anyone who is in doubt as to the nature of his reply can

satisfy his curiosity by going to the arcade in Regent Street near Piccadilly Circus next Poppy Day where for many years past Captain Sarll has been on duty with a collection box.

Tiger's fellow sufferer at Montana's hands, Sergeant Skinner, was a riding instructor who was nicknamed Mrs. Skinner because he had a thin, piping voice.

'Keep your drawers up, Mrs. S., or you'll be in the family way,' the dragoons used to chant in unison as Sergeant Skinner exercised them bareback round the Riding School in the early morning.

'I know who said that,' Sergeant Skinner would shout back. 'If he does it again, I'll have him on a charge. Ter-rot. Canter. Walk march. Down the centre. Dis-mount.'

And that was always the end of it—until next time.

Tiger went on drilling, fighting, shooting, drinking, joking with the R.C.D. till a day came when the regiment had to act as host to a number of young volunteer officers who had come to Toronto for a six-weeks' course. Tiger found himse'f assigned as mentor to a Captain How Cox, a fruit farmer from Cambridge, Nova Scotia.

They liked one another and Captain Cox said to Tiger one day:

'This isn't the life for an educated man like you. Why don't you come and work with me? I'll give you thirty-five dollars a month and you'll live as one of the family. Of course, I'll buy you out, too. How much does it cost?'

'Thirty-five dollars,' Tiger told him—he had good reason to remember the amount.

'A month's pay at my place,' Cox commented. 'Well what do you say?'

'Done,' Tiger replied instantly. He had enjoyed his time with the R.C.D. and is still immensely proud of having served in such a fine regiment. But he had known for some time that his feet were itching again.

7. PIE SOCIAL

WHEN Tiger's discharge came through, he went into the town to draw out his civilian clothes from the store he had parked them in, put them on and then went to get his pay and his discharge papers from the Regimental Sergeant Major.

'Who the devil may you be?' the R.S.M. asked, seeing Tiger for the first time in a frock-coat, grey striped trousers, patent leather boots, spats, grey kid gloves and a top-hat.

Then he noticed the monocle and exploded:

'Gawd Almighty! It's Trooper Sarll. You look like a bloody cabby!'

After a moment, he added, quite seriously:

'Is that why you've left the regiment? To drive a lousy cab?'

Tiger spent the next few days and most of his spare cash giving his cabby's clothes an airing in case he should not have an opportunity to do so in rural Nova Scotia.

When he got to Cambridge, How Cox met him in his buggy and Tiger had his first sight of a real apple orchard parade with battalions of trees dressed like infantry awaiting inspection by, at least, a divisional commander. The Cox family consisted of husband, wife and two small children. There was also a St. Bernard who soon refused to obey anyone but Tiger though nobody seemed to mind, except Tiger who does not hold with dogs obeying one master only unless they are watch dogs, which the St. Bernard quite evidently was not.

The apples on How Cox's estate had just been harvested, and Tiger's main job was to pack them in crates which he stacked on shelves ranging from floor level up to a height of about eight feet.

'Don't you want steps?' How Cox asked him the first morning.

'Why should I?' Tiger replied. 'I'm quite tall enough.'

'But they weigh at least one-and-a-half hundredweight,' Cox objected.

'Is that all?' Tiger said. 'I can manage that easily. At

least, I could when I was with that chap Sparrow. And I can see you're going to feed me better than he did.'

The favourite recreation of the Cambridge folk in those days was known as a Pie Social. Every unmarried girl, young, old, ugly, pretty, fat or thin, baked a pie. When she had done so, she lifted a corner of the crust and pushed in a card bearing her name and address. Then she wrapped it up unrecognizably and took it to the Town Hall. In the evening, the unwrapped pies stood in rows in front of the unmarried men and an auctioneer put them up for sale to the highest bidder who had first to eat the pie, while the assembled company made appropriate comments, and then drive the pie-maker home with equally appropriate comments ringing in both sets of ears as he did so.

Tiger assures me that no decent girl ever told her boy friend which was her pie. On the other hand, there were always people who professed to know. Be that as it may, the bidding and the fun were always as fast as the buyer might subsequently be furious.

Tiger had not been in Cambridge long before he acquired a girl friend in the person of Margaret Caldwell who ran the local post office and who, in addition, possessed a beautiful, shining plait of fair hair right down to a very neat waist. Every afternoon, as soon as Tiger had finished his apple-hoisting, he would hurry to the Post Office and help Margaret sort the letters. On Sundays, he used to accompany her to church.

At Tiger's first Pie Social, one of the local lads said as he was looking at the pies:

'Say, Tiger, I guess I don't have to tell you who made that pie over there.'

'Which one do you mean?' Tiger asked.

'Why, naturally, that one in the green dish.'

'I haven't the slightest idea,' Tiger declared.

'Say, chum, you're kidding,' the other told him. 'We all know you're sweet on her and she's mad about you.'

Tiger smiled.

'I don't know which is Margaret's pie, if that's what you mean,' he confessed. 'I understood she wasn't supposed to tell me, so I didn't ask.'

'Well, if that don't beat the band,' the other remarked. 'I thought you was bound to know that Margaret's is the green one or, for sure, I'd have kept my mouth shut. But it don't matter. You being a greenhorn, it'd be a shame to let you be had for a sucker at your first Pie Social. But don't let on that I told you.'

'Of course I won't,' Tiger promised.

As his eye ranged over the serried ranks of pies he thought of Browning and the rats: Big rats, little rats, brown rats, tawny rats and the rest. The pies looked exactly like that and he smiled again. That green dish with a grey-looking pie: could Margaret really have baked such a thing?

Suddenly he noticed a demure, tawny-topped pie in a willow-pattern dish.

He knew the Caldwells had willow-pattern china. He had eaten off it. Looking once more along the serried ranks of pies, he could see only one in a willow-pattern dish and quickly decided there was going to be no green in his eye that evening.

As he took Margaret home later, she whispered:

'I felt sure you would recognize the dish.'

'I hope you're glad I did,' Tiger told her.

And that, so far as we are concerned, is the end of the matter.

The snow soon lay so thick and inviting that Tiger decided to make himself a toboggan out of some old cheese boxes in the Cox's back yard. A few years later, he would no doubt have made a pair of skis instead. But skis then were still practically unknown outside Scandinavia. Snowshoes were efficient but slow. So Tiger made a toboggan.

One bright, frosty, still night when the moon was full, Tiger invited Margaret and her dear friend, Abby Webster, for a ride. On their way back to the Caldwells' house which stood at the bottom of a steep hill, the left guideline broke.

They were doing at least fifty miles per hour, weaving excitingly between the rows of apple trees in the Caldwells' orchard. There was no hope of stopping till they got to the bottom, but every probability of being stopped.

The toboggan duly dashed itself to bits against the trunk of an apple tree and Tiger did not recover consciousness for some time.

He was lying in the snow and Abby was kneeling beside him.

'Are you all right?' he asked. 'And what's happened to Margaret?'

'I've sent her down to the house,' Abby explained. 'She has cut her nose. I think it's broken.'

'What about you?' Tiger asked again.

'Oh, I'm perfectly all right,' she assured him. 'I just took a header into the snow and all I had to do was to pick myself up. Do you think you can walk down to the house if you put your hand on my shoulder? Or had I better go and get some men to carry you?'

Tiger said he much preferred Abby's shoulder. She was nearly as nice as Margaret, though not so pretty. They were the first girls he had met in Canada who had not only been to school but to College—the first in fact with an intellectual background.

His head buzzed like an angry beehive for a couple of days after the accident but he soon recovered. And, to his intense relief, Margaret's broken nose healed without trace.

By that time winter was nearly over and Tiger's feet were once more pining to move. And they were pointing, like a compass, to London, where Tiger's patent leather boots and spats topped by striped grey trousers, frock-coat and silk hat would not cause him to be mistaken for a cabby.

Yet—and I think it was for the first time—he really hated leaving his friends in Cambridge. He still remembers them with affection and wonders what became of them. But they did not write to him—nor he to them. And their feet have never wandered on to the same path.

He stayed with other friends in St. John's, New Brunswick, whom he had met during the Boer War, and haunted the waterfront to find a ship which would take him back to England. Finally, a harassed captain asked him if he understood cattle. When Tiger said he did, the captain offered him the job of cattle foreman in charge of several hundred steers which he had to ship to Manchester.

The captain omitted to tell Tiger he already had a cattle

foreman. Nor did he tell the first foreman that he had engaged another one. Perhaps he had some excuse—it transpired afterwards that the man was usually drunk.

'Who the bloody hell d'you think you are?' the drunken foreman yelled when he saw Tiger busy organizing the job of getting the steers on board.

'I'm the foreman,' Tiger yelled back. 'And you'll know it if you don't get a move on. Jump to it, man. Head those steers up the gangway, d'you hear. They'll all be on their way back to the prairies in a moment. Or in the water,' he added.

'Do it yourself, you lousy son of a bitch,' the other roared. 'I tell you I'm foreman here. I'll bash your flaming eyeglass into your copulating skull if you try ordering me about.'

'Nonsense, my good man,' Tiger replied. 'I'm the foreman, not you. And you'll damn' well do what I tell you. Pronto. If those beasts break lose, there'll be hell to pay. . . . Here, you other skunks; jump to it or I'll knock your silly blocks together.'

The 'other skunks' had no intention of jumping to anything when they saw every prospect of a fight between the two rival claimants to foremanship and were not sure which would win. So they backed away from the steers and waited.

The original foreman lashed out at Tiger and met Tiger's fist on the way. He went down with a thud and showed no desire to get up again. After that, the other cattlemen gave Tiger no more trouble.

But meanwhile, the steers had got completely out of hand. Some were milling round on the quay. Others rushed madly up the gangway and dashed helter-skelter along the narrow lower deck only to be brought up with a sickening thud and piteous bellow when their wide horns caught against an iron stanchion. Several had their horns wrenched completely off and had to be killed.

The shambles sorted itself out somehow and the voyage started, with Tiger still foreman. Anything further removed from his dream of silk hat, frock-coat and patent leather boots can hardly be imagined. Filthy stalls had to be washed out every day with a hose—and with an even chance of being pinned against the side by the full weight of a steer if the boat rolled. After that, the beasts had to be fed and watered and their wounds attended to.

As if this was not enough, the boat ran into an ice-field off Newfoundland and had to be inched forward for several days before she got clear. Soon the decks and rigging were coated with ice which was often a foot thick and the cattlemen were called in to help chip it off. They chipped off tons, slithering blasphemously about the decks with aching limbs and bleeding fingers. And every time they turned round, the ice seemed to have grown just as thick again as before they chipped it. Before long, they were too tired even to blaspheme.

The boat's name was the *Manchester Trader* and the cattlemen, who ate in the forecastle with the crew, found the food so meagre that they called her the *Manchester Starver* though some had less polite names for her.

There were fourteen cattlemen and they shared a 'cabin' which was about fourteen feet square. In the centre was a coal stove which got red hot as soon as it was replenished. The men never undressed. They simply took off their wet boots and socks and hung them round the stove to dry. Most of the men were sea-sick when they were off duty. Even if there had been a porthole, they could not have opened it: the *Manchester Starver* rolled too much.

The place soon became so fruity that Tiger complained to the captain who turned everybody out and the stove too. Then he turned the hose on. In a couple of days the smell was as bad as before.

Among the cattlemen were a Russian, a Jew, a Cockney (known quite accurately as 'Lousy Jack') and a Turk whom Tiger describes as the best of the bunch.

When at last they reached the Manchester Ship Canal Tiger began to feel a thrill of anticipation. As the vessel steamed along, a section of bridge ahead swung smoothly sideways to let her pass.

'Gawd!' exclaimed Lousy Jack at his side. 'If there ain't a ruddy barge on it!'

For the first time, Tiger felt a sneaking sympathy for Lousy Jack. He knew that if the bridge had carried a road, neither of them would have given it another thought. But another canal—it was unbelievable.

When Tiger had handed the cattle over, he made his way to a public convenience and cleaned himself up in the 'Wash and Brush Up, 2d.' department, as best he could. Then he took a room at the Midland Hotel, put on his cabman's regalia and went out to buy some new underwear, socks and boots. After that, he spent a day or two getting the taste of the *Manchester Starver* out of his mouth and exploring the city, not forgetting the zoo. Having seen all he wanted, he bought a first-class ticket to London. He had no intention of returning in the role of prodigal son.

London was different, somehow. There were more of those wasp-coloured taxis. Fewer hansoms and four-wheelers. More girls on bicycles, looking like animated sand-glasses with their long, wide skirts, narrow waists, padded shoulders and broad-brimmed straw hats.

Tiger arrived on a Saturday evening and spent the night at his father's flat, rather relieved, I think, that his father had retired and was now living at Brighton so that the London flat was empty. Rosa had married and gone to China.

The next morning, Tiger walked rather aimlessly along Piccadilly to Hyde Park. Rotten Row was so colourless that it looked like a morgue. He strolled on, feeling more and more depressed.

Until he found himself at Orators' Corner.

'This is more like it,' he told himself. 'The same old tripe about the British Empire! The same scum talking about it as though it was a cesspool! What do they know about it? Gosh! I must get hold of some of the lads! We'll show 'em!'

8. MAN FRIDAY'S FOOTPRINTS

THE 'lads' were less ready to rally round than Tiger had expected. His best friend, Jack Pilcher, the Bloomsbury dentist, had gone on the journey from which there is no return. Others had married wives and were in process of settling down. It took him quite a while to collect a little band of like-minded sportsmen who were as anxious as he was to take the mickey out of detractors of the British Empire.

Among their butts at Orators' Corner was 'a dirty, long-haired individual' who, besides being a 'Little Englander', passionately insisted that there was no God and that the earth was flat.

'We formed a circle round him,' Tiger wrote afterwards, 'and started to sing hymns. He became very rude, so we suggested he should "get his hair cut" and have a bath. As this didn't stop him, we tipped him and his pulpit over backwards, much to the joy of the crowd, especially the small boys.'

The mickey extractors moved on to another speaker who was enlarging on the Irishman's perennial grievances against the English. Some six hundred people were already milling round him and a fight was in progress. Tiger and his friends shouldered their way through to the platform, pulled down the emerald flag which hung from it and tossed the orator bodily into the struggling mass of humanity beneath.

Having routed the enemy in Hyde Park, they trooped to a hall in which a guild of women socialists were denouncing colonialism, war and the British Empire with special reference to the British Government. At first the 'lads' confined themselves to heckling but when the stewards threw them out, they hailed a passing cab, drove hurriedly to an address Tiger gave in Camden Town and then went back to the hall with a cage containing about two dozen of the largest sewer rats in the dealer's collection.

Telling the cabby to wait, they climbed over some railings, broke a window and emptied the rats into the hall. They did not wait to see what happened, but Tiger wrote that they heard 'a lot of screaming'.

On Boat Race night, they left the British Empire to take care of itself and went off to celebrate a Cambridge victory in Piccadilly Circus where Tiger rounded off a gay evening by standing on his hands, with his opera hat on, in front of the fountain which has since been replaced by Eros.

Another roysterer, a stranger, challenged him.

'I say, ol' sport,' he remarked. 'I'll bet you a fiver you won't walk round that perishin' fountain on your hands without your jolly ol' monocle and opera hat breakin' loose, what?'

'Done,' Tiger said instantly.

'Half a mo',' complained the challenger. 'Lemme finish. Lemme finish, I say. When you've got round, with the ol' eyeglass and whatnot still *in situ*, I'll put a pint pot of beer into your hand and you must drink it while balancing the ol' carcass on your other hand. Comprenny?'

'All right,' Tiger agreed.

He circumnavigated the fountain without a falter and held out his hand for the pint. But when he put the pewter mug to his lips, the beer was scalding hot.

He lost his balance as well as his bet. But he had one consolation: he fell heavily, all sixteen-and-a-half stone of him, on top of the challenger. It was not till the next day that he remembered the scalding beer trick was an old one he ought not to have fallen for.

Possibly it was the scalding beer which was responsible for an idea Tiger and his friends tried out some months later at a Lord Mayor's Show. They hired two windows on different floors overlooking the Strand and, when the usual crowd had collected below, they scattered largesse, consisting of pence and an occasional threepenny bit, out of one of the windows.

The last lot they dropped had been heated on a shovel. The conspirators watched the crowd literally burn its fingers from the other window. But they did not stay there long. The crowd came storming into the building and when it found the empty room began to search elsewhere. The conspirators realized that things were getting too hot for them too and fled hastily down the back stairs to the Embankment.

By this time, Tiger was also beginning to realize that even pence were too valuable to be broadcast in this fashion and he decided to look for a job.

'Why not have a shot at acting?' one of his friends suggested. 'Lots of pretty girls at your feet. Off the stage as well as on. Look at that chap Lewis Waller. He's the rage of London. And Tree. And Henry Irving. Gosh! I'd like to be in their shoes.'

Tiger thought he would, too. So he registered both with Blakemore's Theatrical Agency and with Denton's. Within a week, he had been engaged to play an officer of the United States Army in Claud King's and Violet Luddington's company touring the provinces in *Arizona*, at a salary of £2. 10. 0. a week which was soon raised to £4.

He loved it and went on playing small parts—mostly in the provinces but also in London—for several years. Not continuously, by any means—he frequently exchanged stage dramas for real life ones. He also became involved in films and filming. Sometimes he got the roles mixed up with one another.

As a 'straight' actor, Tiger not only portrayed the U.S. Army ('with knowledge', a critic said) and played a courtier to Lewis Waller's Monsieur Beaucaire, but also led the English soldiery whom Lewis Waller, in the role of King Henry V, urged 'once more into the breach, dear friends'. It was peculiarly appropriate, for Shakespeare makes Henry go on to invite his 'dear friends' to 'imitate the action of the tiger', stiffening their sinews, summoning up their blood and lending their eye a terrible aspect, prying through the portage of the head like the brass cannon.

Tiger says he enjoyed all his parts. But I am sure the one he liked best was baiting awkward theatrical landladies. He was aided and abetted—or, perhaps, egged on—by George Courtney, brother of the more famous Maud Courtney who introduced the song, 'The Honeysuckle and the Bee', to London audiences. She is dead now but Tiger thinks George is still alive. If so, we both hope he will not mind our raking up some of the pranks he and Tiger played in the past.

George and Tiger were about the same age. George had dark, curly hair, large expressive eyes and a humorous mouth from which flowed a stream of eloquent Americanisms which neither Tiger nor I can reproduce in their full flavour.

Tiger insists that both he and George were 'rather shy'. There was certainly an occasion when they hid in a station lavatory to escape the attentions of two pretty Lancashire mill girls in clogs and shawls whom they had rashly invited to tea on the previous day.

The company always put on its best clothes when it moved to the next port of call at the end of the week, and we already know what that meant so far as Tiger was concerned. They were all chatting together waiting for the train when George saw the mill girls bearing down on them.

He and Tiger slunk quickly off to the 'Gentlemen' but were gleefully dragged out by another member of the company and had to walk up and down the platform with their admirers till the train started. George was heard to remark afterwards that he 'felt like ten cents of ice-cream on the end of a red-hot poker'.

'Poker' also happens to have been the nickname George chose for two dour Scottish spinsters with whom he and Tiger, and a third actor, whose name was Alec, lodged at a certain factory town in Lancashire.

The three men had reserved their rooms in advance by letter and were horrified to find when they arrived on the Sunday evening that they were not allowed to smoke, or drink anything stronger than tea.

Worse was to follow on the Monday afternoon. It was the custom of the company to invite the young ladies of the cast to take tea with them in their lodgings before the evening performance. But when the three young ladies whom George, Tiger and Alec had invited rang the bell, the Pokers refused to let them in saying they would not allow 'painted jezebels' to cross their threshold.

The indignant and thwarted hosts protested but the Pokers were adamant. All three would have moved to other lodgings if they could have afforded to. But it would have meant paying double rent. Tiger and Alec were earning £4 a week each, George perhaps more. So they were forced to stay where they were.

On the Saturday morning, when the luggage man came to collect their bags the Pokers refused to let anything leave the house till their bill had been paid.

'But we don't get our salary till after this evening's performance,' the three actors explained. 'We can't pay you till then. We just haven't got the money.'

'Your things don't leave this house till you've paid your bills,' the Pokers repeated firmly.

'But the luggage has to be on the train by midnight,' the three men expostulated. 'We don't get back till after eleven. And your money is perfectly safe because we've got to spend the night here. Our train doesn't leave till ten o'clock to-morrow morning.'

In the end they had to take their luggage to the station in a cab which cost them 9s. 6d. And they only just got it there in time.

Walking back, they discussed reprisals.

'Leave them beldames to me, folks,' George said. 'I'll fix 'em.'

Their tempers were not assuaged when they sat down to supper in the front parlour. While one of the Pokers cooked it in the kitchen, the other sat in the parlour to watch them eat it. She explained that she was not going to give them an opportunity to damage the furniture.

'Our move, I think,' Tiger remarked as he offered his tobacco pouch to George and Alec when they had finished eating.

'My sister and I do not allow smoking,' the Poker reminded them, her corkscrew curls and white lace cap quivering with indignation.

'Now, ain't that just too bad, ma'am,' George remarked as he lit his pipe. And Tiger added: 'You are welcome to try to stop us, madam.'

The other Poker joined her sister soon afterwards, and the three men puffed fast and furiously hoping to smoke the beldames out. But the two spinsters hung on grimly and at last George rose from his chair and said:

'Say, folks, it's hot like red-hot pokers in here. That goddam fire's blazing like all Sodom and Gomorrah. I guess I'll rake it out.'

86

He did so and then threw the window open.

Presently, the two Pokers were so far from red-hot that they were seen to shiver.

'What you need, ma'am, is something to warm you,' George remarked hauling a bottle of beer from his pocket. 'You don't mean to say you won't have some,' he went on, when she glared at him without speaking. 'What about you two boys?' he asked.

Tiger had his own and so had Alec.

'Fine,' George said. 'Now we can make a night of it.'

The two Pokers stuck it a little longer and then retired silently to bed.

After they had gone, the 'theatricals' closed the window and finished their beer. George took out his watch and laid it on the table.

'How long shall we give 'em?' he inquired. 'Ten minutes?'

'Better make it twenty,' Tiger suggested.

'We don't have to wait till them besoms are asleep,' George pointed out. 'You don't imagine they'd let a man see them in their nightdresses, do you? Specially not us. They'd be afraid we'd do 'em wrong.'

'God forbid,' Alec said.

They compromised at a quarter of an hour and then 'got cracking'.

They unwrapped a parcel of kippers they had bought for their Sunday's breakfast, tossed a couple inside the piano, pinned others underneath the table, chairs and sofa and then, happening on a loose floorboard, gleefully slung the rest as far underneath the floor as they could manage so as to make it as difficult as possible to locate them without taking the whole floor up.

'I've an idea, boys,' George remarked, looking thoughtfully at Alec after the last kipper had been disposed of. 'Say Tiger, could you lift the little feller? No, I don't mean just off his feet but over your head. And hold him there. Upside down.'

'Of course,' Tiger replied, stretching out a hand towards Alec.

'Here, I say, what's the idea?' Alec inquired apprehensively.

'It's a real peach,' George declared. 'Just you peel your

boots and socks off, then ooze yourself out of the room and bring me a nice can of water. Good, clean, ordinary water. And for Pete's sake, don't wake them Clytemnestras out of their beauty sleep.'

While the mystified Alec was carrying out his instructions, Tiger watched George pick up the coal shovel, spread a newspaper over the dead fire and carefully scrape down as much soot as he could reach without making a noise. Then he poured the soot on the hearthrug and mixed it into an oozy, black sludge with the water Alec brought from the kitchen.

Having concocted his soot pie, George looked up to see Tiger and Alec grinning appreciatively.

'This ain't nothing,' he told them. 'It's only the make-up. Now we've got to put it on. You peeled them socks off yet, Alec? Fine! Now sit you'self right here. In this nice, cosy, prickly horsehair, straight-laced high-back and wriggle them ugly feet of yours around in this soot pie like you was at the seaside with your mammy wiggling your little toesies in the sand. Tiger's your mammy tonight. And when he judges you've wiggled them little toesies long enough, he'll take you for a walk. Right up one wall, across the ceiling, down the wall on the other side and then across the white table-cloth back to your nice sooty pie. And, if you're good, I 'specs he'll tell you a story.'

After dealing with the parlour, they crept upstairs and did repeat performances in each of their bedrooms. Finally, Alec washed his feet on the parlour carpet, dried them on the antimacassars and put on his socks and boots.

As they let themselves out of the front door, George remarked:

'If them dames don't realize they've had a visit from Robinson Crusoe's Man Friday, they ain't got no imagination.'

Curiously enough, the three Poker-baiters never heard another word about the incident.

The triumvirate split up shortly afterwards. Trouble blazed up in Morocco. Tiger happened to be what the theatrical world calls 'resting'.

There was, in fact, nothing to stop him from going straight out to Tangier.

9. CORRESPONDENT AT WAR

TIGER got the idea of going to Morocco while he was lunching with Monty Dell, the Editor of *Chums*, at the Press Club on 29th July 1907. One of the other guests remarked:

'I suppose you've all heard that the French have just landed an expeditionary force at Casablanca. It looks as if they mean to teach the Sultan of Morocco a lesson.'

'The French are always butting in somewhere,' a journalist complained. 'They would have had the Sudan, and Egypt, in 1898 if Kitchener hadn't been there to tell that Colonel Marchand what's what at Fashoda.'

'There was no Entente Cordiale in those days,' someone else observed. 'Now that the French have agreed to our having a free hand in Egypt, and the Sudan, I suppose it's only fair we should do the same for them in Morocco.'

'If the French are there, it'll keep the Kaiser out,' said another.

'But Morocco is far more important to us than to anybody else,' a man whose name was Colonel Tamplin objected. 'With these modern guns, Gibraltar is already well within range from the Moroccan side of the Straits. What will happen to the Empire if our ships can't use the Straits?'

'That's what I say, sir,' a journalist agreed. 'And why give the Sultan a British military adviser if we're not going to back him?'

'You mean that chap Caid MacLean?' Colonel Tamplin asked. 'The fellow that Moorish brigand, Raisuli, kidnapped. I doubt if the British Government had anything to do with his becoming the Sultan's military adviser. He was only a subaltern in some Scottish Regiment in Gib. when he suddenly threw up his commission and went to live in Tangier. As far as I know he didn't offer his services to the Sultan till some time later.'

'Ah, but why did he go there?' the journalist persisted. 'They were saying in the Lobby last night that he was asked to resign his commission so that he could offer his services to the Sultan in a private capacity—to prevent the French from objecting.'

'Evidently that brigand fellow, Raisuli, thinks MacLean represents the British Government,' another guest observed. 'Otherwise, why kidnap him and then demand £20,000 ransom money from us instead of from the Sultan?'

'Perhaps the Kaiser put him up to it to make trouble between us and the French,' someone suggested.

Tiger, who had been listening with mounting excitement, remarked quietly:

'There's only one way to get to the bottom of it all: go there and see for oneself. How does one get there?'

'You can go out in one of my boats, if you like,' Colonel Tamplin said. 'There's one leaving Southampton the day after tomorrow. For Gib. If that's too soon, there's another on the same day next week.'

'The sooner the better so far as I am concerned,' Tiger replied. 'I'm not doing anything at the moment.'

'Fine,' Colonel Tamplin said. 'Here's my card. Come and see me at my office tomorrow morning and get your ticket.'

'How much will it cost?' Tiger asked, suddenly apprehensive.

"Why, nothing,' Colonel Tamplin told him. 'The boat's half empty, anyway. The only payment I want is a full account of your adventures when you come home. My boats do a lot of business with Morocco and the more I know about what's going on there, the better.'

'I'll certainly do my best, sir,' Tiger promised.

'Why don't you get into touch with one of the dailies before you go?' Monty Dell suggested. 'Morocco's very much in the news, what with the Raisuli-MacLean affair, French intrigues in Fez and now the landing at Casablanca.'

'Won't they send their own men out, in that case?' Tiger asked.

'Some will, certainly,' his host agreed.

'I'm afraid I haven't time to find out which will not,' Tiger said. 'I'll have to go out first and see how the land lies. But it's an excellent idea.'

Somebody else remarked that there would be a good market for pictures so Tiger spent seventy pounds on the latest thing in cameras, a portable developing outfit and a large supply of plates.

They were stolen from him in Tangier and he replaced them with a Brownie which would have cost him five shillings in London but which he had to pay £2. 10. 0. for to a Moorish merchant in the Souk. However, his pictures netted him £400 altogether, so he did not do so badly.

The ferryboat from Gibraltar duly decanted him at Tangier where he booked a room at McLean's Hotel which appears to have had no connexion with the Caid MacLean who had been kidnapped by Raisuli. The manager was friendly and advised him to get into touch with R. L. N. Johnson, the local correspondent of the *Morning Post*.

Tiger found Johnson a charming, bearded, middle-aged man who spoke fluent Arabic, French and Spanish and who reminded him of Charles Dickens. Johnson's interests were political and, at his time of life, he had no desire to become a war correspondent. He also had a shrewd idea that the only way to get news to London from Casablanca was to have someone in Tangier who would send it on. He cabled his editor to this effect and Tiger was a fully-fledged war correspondent by the following morning. It is perhaps worth mentioning that he had no passport. One did not bother about such things before World War I, unless one was going to Russia or Turkey.

Tiger's next problem was how to get to Casablanca. It was impossible to go by land, and ships only called there very occasionally. But he found out by chance that a British torpedo-boat was going there on the following day so he went to ask if she would come to his rescue.

The officer who commanded her drew himself up and replied:

'My good fellow! The Royal Navy is not at the disposal of Fleet Street scribblers.'

Lying within a cable's length of the British warship was a French torpedo-boat, the *Balliste*, so Tiger told his boatman to take him there.

The French captain, who spoke passable English, replied: 'Why, of course,' when Tiger posed the same question. He added:

'We leave in two hours. Can you make it?'

'Most certainly, captain,' Tiger replied. 'I am extremely grateful to you.'

'The French Navy is always at your disposal,' the captain declared.

During the voyage, Tiger learnt that two French torpedo-boats, *Balliste* and *Arquebus*, were constantly commuting between Tangier and Casablanca and that he was welcome to use either of them—the cruiser *Gloire*, too—whenever he liked.

'All you have to do,' the captain explained, 'is to get yourself accredited to the French Foreign Legion at Casablanca and we will carry you wherever you wish to go. Your messages, too.'

'Do you mean I can go anywhere?' Tiger asked incredulously. 'Not just to Tangier and back?'

'Why, of course,' the captain said. 'Provided there is a naval ship going there. As a member of the Foreign Legion you will be entitled to call on the French Navy at all times. And you do not have to pay.'

Accreditation in those days meant that Tiger was regarded not merely as a correspondent but also as a sort of supernumerary combatant. So, in due course, and to his delight, he acquired a rifle—a French Martini Henry—and the usual concomitants.

When he reached Casablanca, he found that only one British correspondent had preceded him—Charles E. Hands, the famous war correspondent of the *Daily Mail*. He had beaten all the rest to it, including such men as Bennett Burleigh —a tall man who rode everywhere on a minute donkey— Ashmead Bartlett who married the Baroness Burdett Coutts, the first woman ever to write a cheque for a million pounds and a former neighbour of Tiger's parents at Highgate when he used to fire ink pellets at Georgina Jack's panties.

All these men are dead now. Indeed, I think the only survivor besides Tiger is David McLellan who went out to take photographs for the *Daily Mirror*.

The two met as David stepped ashore when Tiger had gone to see if *Arquebus* had brought any letters for him.

'My name is Tiger Sarll of the *Morning Post*,' he said to the newcomer. 'Have a cigar?'

Recalling the scene more than half a century after, David said:

'I was pretty young then and I can honestly say I have never seen such an extraordinary chap before or since. He was about as tall as I would have been on stilts. He was half in uniform and half in civvies. He wore a monocle and had a rifle slung across his shoulder with several notches on the stock. He was also carrying a stick which I discovered later was a swordstick. I suppose the notches represented the Moors he had shot but I didn't like to ask him. Yes, and that cigar. It was perfectly frightful. I threw it away as soon as I could without his seeing. Afterwards I wished I hadn't—you couldn't get a smoke for love or money.'

After telling Tiger his name, David asked him which hotel he should go to.

'There aren't any,' Tiger replied. 'But there are only about five hundred inhabitants left out of twenty thousand, so one just plants oneself in an empty house. Personally, I find all the houses so filthy that I'm camping on a roof. There's plenty of room if you would care to join me.'

'You're sure you don't mind?' David inquired.

'Of course not,' Tiger assured him. 'Come along and I'll show you where it is. Then, if you like, I'll take you round to the Foreign Legion headquarters so that you can arrange about your accreditation. I'm going there anyway.'

'Why do I have to do that?' David asked.

'You won't be able to send off your dispatches unless you're accredited,' Tiger explained.

'But I don't want to send any dispatches,' David objected. 'I'm a photographer.'

'I'll bet you'll have to have a permit, all the same,' Tiger said.

But it was not so simple as that.

'My instructions,' Major Mangin of the French Foreign Legion explained, 'are to accredit war correspondents who present proper credentials from their employers. There is not a word, not a single word, about photographers. I am very sorry.'

'It's not fair,' David protested indignantly. 'What it amounts to is, if I were a correspondent, I could send out as many photographs as I liked simply by calling them dispatches. But, as I'm a photographer, I can't send out anything: no dispatches; no photographs. I suppose I can't even send myself out.'

'Technically, you ought not to have been allowed to send yourself in,' Major Mangin corrected. 'But you are here and I daresay we could arrange to send you back to Tangier provided you took no photographs or dispatches with you.'

'Hell!' David said.

'What would happen if I appointed Mr. McLellan as my assistant?' Tiger inquired.

Major Mangin burst out laughing.

'An excellent idea, my friend,' he said. 'How do you spell the name?'

Tiger and David hunted as a team for the rest of the campaign. Tiger provided the cover and David paid in photographs so that the Brownie was not wholly responsible for the unexpected windfall of four hundred pounds Tiger found waiting for him when he got back to London.

When Tiger arrived in Casablanca, the Moors were still besieging the town and the French forces were making frequent sorties with the object of enlarging the perimeter. Tiger went with them whenever he could—he enjoyed fighting much more than writing dispatches about fighting.

Once, when the French were withdrawing after an attack of this kind, the Moors cut off their rearguard, Tiger with it. There was a running fight during which all the French were shot down one after the other. The last to die were two officers who embraced and then charged the Moors, shouting '*Vive la France*' as they ran firing their revolvers till they fell mortally wounded.

Their gallantry probably saved Tiger's life by drawing the Moors' fire and distracting their attention. Taking advantage of the respite, he made a dash for a small tower which stood about a hundred yards away. The Moors were soon in full cry after him but their shots went wide and he reached the tower without a scratch.

The door was a flimsy affair, not worth trying to barricade, but Tiger saw a staircase and raced up it on to a flat roof round which ran a low parapet. And, some thirty to forty feet

Tiger's father—John Thomas Sarll, B.A.

At the age of nine, Tiger was given this grass snake by Mary Kingsley: already he was five feet eleven inches tall—nine inches taller than his father

A general view of Tangier as Tiger found it in 1905

A typical street in Buenos Aires at the beginning of the century. Tiger arrived there in 1910

Our War Pictures

We have altogether eight expert staff Photographers at the Front, covering every point of interest on both Sides.

Capt. T. W. H. SARLL

IN CAMP AT CHORLU. *By courtesy of Central News.*

One of our Special Correspondents with the Turkish Army, whose magnificent Pictures of the War have caused so much sensation.

EXTRACTS FROM SOME OF CAPT. SARLL'S RECENT LETTERS AND CABLES FROM THE FRONT—

Letter dated Constantinople, November 10th.

"I have just come in from the front in order to get into touch with you and get my stuff off without the Censor seeing it, and last but not least to get something to eat."

"I have been smashed up once or twice. The greatest trouble I have to contend with is the matter of servants. None of them will stay with me. In Constantinople they were very anxious to see some fighting, but the moment the first shell burst they were off like a couple of Marathon runners."

"At Lule Burgas I had to carry the Camera complete for three days and three nights."

"I have had to bolt away from the *dear old lady* who nurses the correspondents, otherwise should not be able to get into the fighting line."

Letter dated November 19th.

"I am at a place called Derkas on the extreme Turkish right flank; there are as yet no other correspondents here as they do not know that fighting is going on. I have cleared off on my own, and the headquarter staff don't know where

to find me. All the other correspondents are penned up with a nurse in Constantinople. I have sent you some stuff by this mail which I hope you will like. I have not wired the titles as the Censor would see my telegram and find out that I have got through the lines and send orders for me to be arrested. A special dispatch rider goes to Constantinople for my letters and with my films, so you are now pretty sure to get the stuff O.K."

"The papers say that during the last 5 days there has been no fighting but they are *quite wrong*, I have just been 5 days in the saddle, and present during the last 5 days at the most murderous fighting on the right flank. The Bulgars are massing on Derkas Lake and are going to fight their way through the right flank."

Cable received November 26th.

"I leave for Kilios to-morrow, thence Derkas, Hademkeui, Chatalja, and as near Bulgar lines as possible, very difficult getting pictures, no correspondents allowed at front, have to dodge. Cannot get servants stay with me, run away when shelled. Camera body draws enemy's fire, mistaken for maxim. No fighting last 6 days, Bulgars tired, Turks in strong position. Only four correspondents at front all time, rest in Constantinople."

A page of Captain Sarll's dispatches home from the front during the Balkan War in 1912

'A Show Worth Seeing': a poster for 'Rais' Sarll's circus

'Rais' Sarll with two of his snakes. (*Above*), with a venomous horned snake in 1927, and (*below*), with a nineteen-foot python at Bertram Mills' Circus in 1935

Tiger in 1928, wearing reindeer-skin gloves to handle a newly arrived member of his circus (*above*), and putting a three-foot alligator to sleep by hypnosis (*below*)

Captain and Mrs. Sarll at their home at Bradwell-on-Sea, Essex, and (*below*), Tiger as B.B.C. Television viewers saw him with Éamonn Andrews in the 'This is Your Life' programme

below, on the side farthest from his pursuers, there was a shed with a thatched roof.

Tiger instantly climbed over the parapet and jumped, feet foremost, his Martini-Henry held close to his side. The thatch filled his eyes, nose and throat with dust but it held and when he picked himself up he found he was unhurt. So was the Martini-Henry.

In front of him was an open space beyond which was the entrance to a lane, flanked by buildings and apparently leading towards the town, presumably to one of the gates where there was a French guard-post. If he could get to the lane, he should be safe. But could he?

He could hear his pursuers yelling as they searched the tower for him. Then the yells redoubled and a bullet zipped wickedly into the thatch as he jumped to the ground and ran for the lane.

He got there safely and the Moors withdrew without trying to follow him.

On another occasion, General Drude, who commanded the French forces, invited the British journalists to take part in a night attack on a Moorish stronghold called Tedurt which appears to have been some twenty miles from Casablanca.

The French general was a short, bow-legged man who spoke excellent English.

'The point of departure,' he told Tiger and his 'assistant', David McLellan, 'is outside the main gate and we move off at two a.m. precisely.'

'What about the curfew?' Tiger asked. 'We don't want to be shot while getting there.'

'If you carry a lantern, all right,' General Drude told them. 'Without it, pouf! You will be shot. Perhaps they will ask questions after. But not of you!'

Even if they had been able to find lanterns, there was no paraffin. All they were able to scrounge was one tallow candle which they cut in half and stuck into two jam jars. They had only gone a few yards when both halves blew out.

'Damn this wind,' Tiger remarked as he relit them. 'How many matches have you got, David?'

David had five and Tiger two, one of which blew out as he

was trying to get it into the neck of the jam jar without burning his fingers. By the time they reached the gate, they had used the lot.

And then the sentry refused to let them through.

He did not relent till they thought of offering him a five-franc piece—worth four shillings in those days.

The column had moved off by the time they reached the rendezvous but one of the mules had obligingly left a memento which showed them which way to go. The Foreign Legion marched at a sort of jog-trot which took it along at nearly five miles an hour but they caught the column up at last. When Major Mangin saw them, he said:

'So there you are! I thought you had thought better of coming.'

It was a cold, clear night and the dust was appalling. Tiger and David tied their handkerchiefs over their mouths and noses but their teeth felt like millstones in action all the same.

The column reached the deployment point just before dawn and found that the Moors were expecting them. The assault had to be made across a ravine which was enfiladed from both flanks and the Moors kept up a constant, but not very accurate fire whenever they saw anything moving.

Tiger, armed with his rifle and David with his camera, ran across between two mules which were carrying boxes of small arms ammunition and were also extremely worried at the noise that was going on all round them. They lashed out at anything in reach and mules can reach a surprisingly long way. Fortunately, they failed to damage either David or Tiger and the Moorish bullets were considerate enough not to embed themselves in the boxes of ammunition. If they had done so, Tiger's toast to women and gunpowder would undoubtedly have come true.

Tiger rounded off his reminiscences of the occasion by remarking that it was the first time David had been under fire, that he was only twenty-one and hadn't turned a hair. When I mentioned this to David, he remarked: 'Didn't I? The only thing I really remember is riding back to Casablanca on a gun carriage after it was all over. When we got to the gate, we ran

into Maxwell of the *Daily Mail* who greeted us with the remark:
'"Hullo, you chaps, where've you been?"

'I told him we had got mixed up in a battle to which he replied: "You look like it. I expect you could both do with a dish of char. Come along to my place and I'll see what I can do."'

Char was a luxury in Casablanca and David says they both drank at least a gallon. It was almost as difficult to get drinking water as it was to get tea. Most of the wells had dead bodies in them. A good many of them were Moroccan Jews whom the Moors had attacked from one side on the ground that they sympathized with the French, while the French fired from the other because they were dressed like the Moors.

Owing to the scarcity of water, when Tiger washed it was generally in wine which he also had to drink though it was like vinegar. Food was as scarce as water and there were many days on which Tiger had nothing to eat but raw potatoes.

The French soldiers were on short commons, too. What food they had was prepared for them by women whom Tiger says were called *vivandières* though they seem to have been something between nurses and A.T.S., not camp followers. One of them gave him a wooden wine flask which he still has.

He was carrying a Moorish girl in his arms when they met. He had found the girl lying in the street, groaning with the first pangs of child-birth. He lifted her up and carried her to a nearby French post where he knew there was generally a doctor. But the doctor had been called away and the baby was born with the help of the *vivandière* and two French soldiers. After it was over, the *vivandière* unclipped the flask which was hanging at her waist and offered Tiger a drink. When he handed the flask back, she told him to keep it. He never saw her again.

Soon after Tiger's arrival, the French brought a captive observation balloon to Casablanca. As the Moors watched it gradually swelling and rising from the ground they fell to the earth shouting '*afreet*', which means 'devil', instead of firing at it. Nevertheless, the balloon caught fire and was destroyed and it was some time before another arrived from France. This time it was inflated successfully and squads of Legionaries then had to tow it up and down behind the front line while its occupants signalled the enemy's position to the French artillery.

It is to be hoped that their messages had more effect than one which Tiger says was delivered in his hearing to an Infantry officer directing his company's fire against a target some four hundred yards away.

'*Mon capitaine*,' said a breathless and agitated soldier. 'I have been sent to tell you that those are our Spahis you are firing at.'

'*Qu' importe?*' replied the officer—and went on firing.

Thanks, perhaps, to the observation balloon, if not to the nameless captain, the Moors were gradually pushed farther and farther away from the town and their line ceased to be continuous. Use of the balloon after that merely warned the Moors of impending attacks, so the '*afreet*' was deflated and sent home.

The more Tiger saw of the Casablanca affair, the less he liked it. The trouble began because the French insisted on laying a small temporary railway line through a corner of a Moslem graveyard. The Moslems regarded this as desecration and took up arms when the French refused to re-site the line.

With goodwill, it would have been so easy to avoid the cemetery that Tiger believes the French authorities deliberately picked a quarrel to give them an excuse to strengthen their hold on Morocco—and, indeed, they dethroned one Sultan and imposed another just at that time.

Tiger's version of the facts was sent to the *Morning Post* by Johnson and resulted in awkward questions being asked in Parliament. They vindicated the right of free speech but had no other effect whatsoever.

The tribesmen round Casablanca gave up the unequal struggle after a while and the British war correspondents drifted away one by one. Most of them went back to London but Tiger stayed in Tangier.

He was determined to try to solve the mystery of Raisuli and Caid MacLean.

Johnson was dubious at first about letting him go.

'Raisuli is a tough egg,' he objected. 'If he took a dislike to you, you might come back minus your ear. Or, you mightn't come back at all.'

'I wouldn't blame you in either case,' Tiger said.

'Perhaps not! But the old *Morning Post* might,' Johnson pointed out. 'I'm its official representative here. If I send you to interview Raisuli, I do so on behalf of the paper. And if you don't come back, there'll be hell to pay—questions in Parliament and all that. We've had enough of them already over your Casablanca story. You know the one I mean. And this time, you'd be an international incident. I won't risk it.'

'But surely there could be no objection to my going to see Raisuli on my own and selling the story to you for the *M.P.* when I get back—if I do get back, of course,' Tiger persisted.

'I suppose not,' Johnson admitted after a short pause. 'No, you're a free agent. A bit mad, but still. . . . But you'll have to do the whole thing on your own. I mustn't come into it. Is that clear?'

'Perfectly,' Tiger said. 'Provided you'll tell me how to set about it.'

'You had better go and see a merchant in the Souk,' Johnson advised. 'His name is Ibrahim Moghraby. He speaks English. Anybody will tell you where to find him.'

'I am told you can help me to meet Raisuli,' Tiger said when he had traced him.

'Who told you such a lie?' Ibrahim asked, without passion.

'Mr. Johnson,' Tiger explained.

'Why did you not say so in the beginning?' Ibrahim asked. 'For Mr. Johnson, I would even try to move heaven as well as earth. Maybe, I can help him in this matter also. If so, I shall send him word.'

'Send it to me, not him,' Tiger urged.

'If he wishes you to be informed, he will inform you,' Ibrahim

99

replied. 'But who am I to presume to know what his wishes are?'

Tiger realized then that the merchant did not intend to commit himself before he had made sure that his unknown visitor really did come from Johnson. So he did not press the matter.

He spent the next three days exploring Tangier, especially the Souk with its filthy, tumble-down booths between which meagre, over-laden donkeys, gaunt cats, a few mangy curs and a seething mass of ragged, poverty-stricken human beings jostled against one another and bargained interminably with over-fed merchants who alternately poured out torrents of impassioned words or sat, impassively smoking, seemingly not caring whether they sold their wares or not.

When Tiger had seen enough of the Souk, Johnson advised him to pay a visit to the prison which he found at the top of a steepish hill near the Kassabeh Gate. It was a long, low, evil-looking place which ran the whole length of a large courtyard. Its great door, studded with iron nails, lay in a dark passage. Two old, fat, armed negroes guarded the entrance to the passage and demanded baksheesh before they would let Tiger past. Two more made the same demand when he reached the door.

When he had complied with the second demand, one of the negroes led him to the door and slid back an iron panel which covered a small hole through which he invited Tiger by signs to put his head.

Tiger did so and his nostrils were at once filled with a foetid stench which rivalled that from the dead elephant in Rhodesia. Then outstretched claws clutched at his cheeks, forehead, mouth, while whining voices begged for alms in Arabic or implored him with signs to buy pathetic little knick-knacks which his guide told him the prisoners made in the hope of selling them to buy food.

Beyond these importunate wretches lay others, unable to move because their legs were encased in heavy chains, but equally vocal and even more pathetic.

Tiger extricated himself as soon as he could.

'Doesn't the Government feed them?' he asked first.

'No, only their relatives,' the guide replied.

'And if they have none?'

'Tourists, like your honour, give them baksheesh or buy what they have for sale.'

'And when there are no tourists?'

'It is in the hands of Allah.'

'Tell the guard to open the grill,' Tiger said.

He tossed in some coins and the clamour they aroused sickened him more than the stench. He wished he had not gone there. Then he told himself that the only way to cure such evils was to bring them to light.

In due course, Ibrahim came to see him at his hotel.

'Do you still wish to make the journey of which we spoke?' the Moor asked.

'I certainly do,' Tiger replied.

'Can you start tomorrow, at daybreak?'

'The sooner the better,' Tiger declared.

'It would be impolite to go empty-handed,' Ibrahim remarked. 'Therefore I shall provide three asses: one for each of us to ride and the third for our food and the gifts.'

Tiger had forgotten about gifts. 'What do you think Raisuli would like?' he inquired.

'Something from Europe,' Ibrahim advised.

Tiger's pocket was by no means bottomless, Tangier prices by no means low and the choice extremely limited. In the end, he decided on a large German clock of imitation marble and a pair of field glasses which he had the good fortune to pick up from an English sailor he happened to meet in the Souk. He did not think it advisable to inquire where they came from.

The patient asses carried Ibrahim, Tiger and their chattels sedately out through the Water Front Gate and then along desolate valleys and over rock-ribbed hills till nightfall when Ibrahim called a halt between two low hills carpeted with wild geraniums in full bloom. There was a village nearby but they did not enter it.

Ibrahim washed, spread a mat on the ground and said his prayers facing Mecca as the Islamic religion demands. Then he cooked their supper and fed the asses after which the two men lay down on the bare ground and slept. At dawn, Ibrahim awoke, washed and prayed again and they both breakfasted.

'I shall leave you now,' Ibrahim said to Tiger when they had finished. 'Stay with the two asses and God till I return. Do not enter the village. If children come and plague you, drive them away.'

'If I know anything about children,' Tiger objected, 'they will come back.'

'Not if you make this sign,' Ibrahim told him, raising his right hand and extending the first finger. Then he turned his wrist over and back quickly several times.

'What does it mean?' Tiger asked as he tried to copy the gesture.

'Nay, keep the forearm steady,' Ibrahim instructed. 'Turn the wrist only. Thus. . . . Ah, that is better. And the meaning? It is a protection against the eye of Iblis, the Evil One. You will see that it—protects. Against children also. Even against their fathers.'

It worked like a charm. Indeed, in a sense, it is one— throughout the world of Islam. But it is much less effective today than it was when Tiger (and I, too) learnt of it half a century ago.

The day passed eerily as well as wearily. There were birds of prey wheeling overhead and strange noises came sometimes from the hills. The children gathered as Ibrahim had predicted—a ragged, motley lot, many with one eye sightless through trachoma and both eyes festooned with flies. Others were pitted from smallpox. Many had festering sores on their legs and arms. All looked half starved and all came begging. But they melted away quickly at the sight of Tiger's minatory forefinger. Some of the bolder ones came back several times, though at increasingly long intervals. After midday, no one came near him. He lay and smoked and the two asses, hobbled, moved with little, ungainly jumps in search of grass. Sometimes Tiger took them water which he drew from a well near where they had slept.

As the hours dawdled by, Tiger wondered what he would do if Ibrahim did not come back. He had not the slightest idea where he was and he could not ask for he knew no Arabic, and, at that time, only a few words of Spanish which some of the Moors in the north spoke haltingly.

His doubts were resolved when Ibrahim returned during the afternoon with another Moor who was on foot, spoke no English and carried a rifle.

'It can be arranged,' Ibrahim said. 'But on one condition only: that you play chess. Do you play chess?'

'Yes,' Tiger replied. 'Why?'

'It is good,' Ibrahim said, without answering the question. 'It is also good that I spoke the truth without knowing that I did so. Allah be praised.'

He spoke volubly to the other Moor in Arabic, committed Tiger and the guide to the care of God and said he would wait with the asses for Tiger's return.

The armed Moor led Tiger on foot along a stony path in the winding valley. Then they climbed the steep hillside and came to a halt outside a cave the entrance to which was guarded by several armed men.

Tiger's guide made signs to him to wait and disappeared into the cave from which came sounds which Tiger felt sure were made by bagpipes. He thought he must be dreaming.

Presently the guide returned and beckoned Tiger to follow him into the cave. It was dimly lit and smoky and had a strange smell in which sweat and incense predominated.

The skirl of the pipes grew louder and then ceased abruptly.

'Who the devil are you and what the hell do you want?' a voice asked, in English.

'I'm a journalist,' Tiger explained. 'I have come to try to get to the bottom of the Caid MacLean affair.'

'Hm!' said the other. 'So you're one of those Fleet Street meddlers. I might have guessed it. . . . Well, I'm Caid MacLean. But I'm damned if I know what business it is of yours.'

'The British public . . .' Tiger began.

'To hell with that,' MacLean interrupted. 'What's your paper?'

'The *Morning Post*,' Tiger replied somewhat acidly.

'Oh!' MacLean remarked. 'Well, go back and tell your

Editor that you've spoken to me: that I'm perfectly well and that you interrupted my playing the pipes.'

'So it was you,' Tiger said.

'Who else do you think it could have been?' MacLean asked.

'I would like to ask you about the ransom,' Tiger began. 'How much does Raisuli really want? And why has he asked the British Government to pay instead of asking the Sultan? What will happen to you if the British Gov——'

'Young man,' Caid MacLean broke in, 'if you must ask silly questions, ask Raisuli to answer them, not me. I don't suppose he will for one moment. He is just as likely to put a price on you as on me. What do you think the *Morning Post* would pay?'

'Nothing,' Tiger replied promptly. 'Actually I wasn't sent here. I just came.'

'That's the first sensible thing you've said since you arrived,' MacLean observed. 'If Raisuli thought he could make money by keeping you here, you wouldn't have an outside chance of getting away again. If you're not worth holding, he may let you go. He isn't interested in chicken feed. He's playing for big stakes. So, as it happens, am I. That's why I came here. Anyway, it's high time I went and told him what you're here for. Stay exactly where you are till I come back.'

When MacLean had gone, Tiger tried to sort out his impressions. He still has not decided what MacLean meant. Were the 'high stakes' political or merely £20,000 which Raisuli and MacLean intended to share? Was some European Power behind Raisuli and, if so, which? And why ask the British Government to pay the ransom seeing that MacLean was an employee of the Sultan of Morocco? Was it simply because Raisuli knew the Sultan would not pay and believed that the British Government would? Or was that chap in the Press Club right when he suggested that the Kaiser had put Raisuli up to it in order to make trouble between Britain and France?

Whatever the object of the exercise was, the affair petered out. MacLean was actually released when the British Government had paid, not the £20,000 Raisuli originally demanded, but an 'instalment' of £4,000, and promised Raisuli their 'protection', a word which could have involved us in war if it was meant seriously—Raisuli was always in trouble with either the Spaniards, the French or the Sultan; often with all three. When the next instalment of the ransom money fell due, the British Government refused to pay, on the ground that Raisuli's behaviour did not warrant it. Then the Foreign Office wasted much time and paper trying to persuade the Spanish Government to pay the money back on the theory that the incident had occurred in what was then known as 'the Spanish Zone' of Morocco. In the end, Whitehall gave it up.

MacLean came back to Tiger after a while and told him that Raisuli was not prepared to be interviewed. It seemed, in fact, that Raisuli had been told that Tiger simply wished to challenge him to a game of chess and was highly annoyed to find that the challenge was a mere subterfuge. However, if Tiger did play chess after all, Raisuli was prepared to overlook the offence provided that Tiger would promise not to publish anything about what he had seen or heard.

'What shall I tell him?' MacLean asked finally.

'I haven't much choice, have I?' Tiger remarked.

'No,' MacLean replied shortly. 'I suppose you do play chess?'

'Oh, yes,' Tiger said.

'Then you had better come along and I'll introduce you,' MacLean advised. 'I don't know how good a player you are, but Raisuli rather fancies himself. And he doesn't like losing.'

'I understand,' Tiger replied. 'By the way, I've brought a couple of small presents with me. What shall I do with them?'

'Trot them out after I have presented you,' MacLean told him.

Tiger only saw Raisuli in the dim light of the cave. He thinks of him as short, bull-necked, broad and hairy—a regular Esau of a man with a flaming red beard (possibly reddened with henna) which covered the whole of his face except for a narrow rim between his nose, little dark eyes and turban. The eyes looked hostile but they seemed to relax a little when Tiger bowed and proffered the clock and they quite definitely lit up when he held out the field glasses.

After accepting the gifts, Raisuli clapped his hands and a Berber slave brought a tray with mint tea in greeny-yellow

Venetian tumblers decorated with a gold rim and gold flowers. It was green tea, very sweet and possibly with a hint of ambergris.

When they had drunk the tea, Caid MacLean left them and the slave then brought a chessboard with squares of inlaid ivory and ebony. The ivory men fascinated Tiger who loves beautiful things. He had never seen their like before. Each of the pieces represented a Moroccan tribe. Half had white *jellabas* (long cloaks) and turbans, the other half brown.

Tiger found Raisuli a better player than he had expected—quite good enough to have resented an obvious blunder made to let him win: not quite good enough to beat Tiger if both went all out for victory.

They drank many more cups of mint tea and played two games which Tiger lost—apparently without arousing Raisuli's suspicions that he had lost deliberately. Then Tiger was conducted to a pile of rugs and went to sleep. He did not see either MacLean or Raisuli again.

When Tiger got back to Tangier, he told Johnson in confidence what had transpired. Soon afterwards he went back to London and told Colonel Tamplin. Fifty-five years later, he told me.

Having collected his money from the *Morning Post*, he spent some of it on a seven horse-power Sunbeam motor-cycle with a basket trailer. It had no gears and the batteries kept on corroding with the result that Tiger got stranded in the most inconvenient places.

That basket trailer seems to have set him thinking. Sometimes it had a passenger in it—more often not. When it was empty, he felt lonely.

He came to the conclusion that it was time he got married. But, to whom?

Tiger was twenty-five now and his father had been saying for years that it was time he thought about settling down and raising a family.

Tiger is one of those people who are ready to try everything more than once, even including settling down. As for marriage: well, he had thought of it many times but, when it came to the point of proposing, he had always shied off. It was certainly not for want of encouragement on the part of the opposite sex— I have been told by one of them that the girls flocked round him like protons round a nucleus. She said she felt so sorry for him that she decided to marry him herself. And she did.

Tiger's search for a wife narrowed by degrees to a house inhabited by Mr. and Mrs. Athelstan Smith and a large family of boys and girls. One of these, known as 'Kissy', had been a successor to Georgina of the ink-spotted panties as Tiger's 'best girl'. This was before he went to fight the Boers and he had never seen her since. He suddenly began to wonder what she was like now she was grown up.

Wasting no time, he jumped on to his motor-cycle and took its empty trailer straight down to her house where he arrived in the midst of the devil's own thunderstorm.

'Just what I needed,' Tiger said to himself—he had been racking his brains all the way from London to find a plausible excuse for his visit.

The storm conveniently drenched him to the skin, so he rang the bell and said to the maid who answered it:

'I wonder if Mrs. Athelstan Smith would mind if I came in and dried myself—I happened to be passing and this storm has made me wet through. She used to know my mother, Mrs. Sarll, in London. Will you tell her that it is Willie Sarll.'

Mrs. Smith came herself to welcome him and he brought the conversation round to Kissy as soon as he considered tactful.

'Yes, she is at home,' her mother said in answer to his inquiry. 'But it's no use asking her to come down and meet you. She has taken an unaccountable and foolish dislike to men and always locks herself in her room whenever a man comes to the house. . . . Ah, but here's Sybil. Sybil, my dear, this is Willie Sarll. I daresay you remember, he used to be Kissy's beau when we lived in Bloomsbury, oh, years ago.'

Tiger looked down at Sybil, who about came up to his armpits, and forgot all about Kissy. Next time he went, he was immaculate from his monocle down to his spats and patent leather boots and gold topped malacca.

Sybil approved of his wooing but the rest of the family weighted the scales heavily in the other direction. While the issue was still in the balance, Mr. Athelstan Smith died suddenly from heart failure while on the way to the Stock Exchange of which he was a member. Sybil read about it in the evening paper before the news reached her family and rushed home to break it gently to her mother.

Some months afterwards, Tiger again rode his motor-cycle up to the door, Sybil stepped into the trailer and they drove away to London to be married. They had made no secret about it and when they arrived at the Registrar's Office in Henrietta Street, near Covent Garden, they found a posse of Sybil's brothers waiting outside the door.

'You're to come home with us,' they told Sybil. 'You aren't of age yet and can't marry unless Mother agrees. Well, she doesn't. So come along.'

'What am I to do?' Sybil asked Tiger tearfully.

'Why, get married of course,' he replied. Then he turned to the brothers and added: 'Would you please stand away from that door. Sybil and I are due inside.'

'She's coming home with us,' they told him.

Tiger lifted Sybil's hand off his arm.

'Look here, you chaps,' he remarked pleasantly. 'I'm quite good with my fists, you know. I don't suppose you want a schimozzle on the pavement any more than I do, especially as I can assure you that anyone I hit generally lies down for quite a long while. So I suggest you either move away from that door or, better still, shake hands and come and be witnesses at the wedding. I can spare you one minute to make up your minds.'

The brothers looked at one another, and grinned.

'It's all right,' they said. 'You win. We told Mother it wouldn't be any use trying to stop you. But she insisted. She said Father wouldn't have let you marry Sybil. She's quite right, you know. He wouldn't.'

After the ceremony, and the wedding breakfast, they all went back to Sybil's home together. The newly-married pair stayed with the Smiths for a while and then moved to Mr. Sarll's London flat where they tried to make up their minds what to do and where to do it. A somewhat less newly-married couple, a Mr. and Mrs. Algy Birkett, suggested that Sybil should keep house for them and she agreed, though at that time she knew almost less about house-keeping than she did of marriage about which she had known nothing beyond the fact that after a girl changed her name she was styled 'Mrs.' and a stork came over from Holland with a series of babies. She had never been to school and her governesses had not seen fit to enlighten her further—as spinsters they were not expected to know. And her mother appears to have been too shy.

Mr. and Mrs. Birkett were a delightful couple. He was a barrister. In process of time he became a judge, a very famous one. But he plays no further part in our story.

After a while, Tiger got bored with night starvation and one day he said to Sybil:

'Lewis Waller says there's a part for me in *The White Man* on tour. And for you. What about it?'

Of course Sybil agreed, but without enthusiasm. She told me she hated the stage—that she shivered, not with excitement, but real fear every time she had to go on, even when she had no lines to speak. But she adored careering through the English countryside at week-ends. Tiger had sold the motor-cycle by this time and their means of locomotion was the traditional bicycle for two newly-weds who, in this case, measured respectively five feet one inch and six feet four.

They always cycled from one town to the next instead of going by train like the rest of the company and the manager added their train fare to their salaries so that the journey cost them less than nothing. Tiger loved the exercise: Sybil the chance to devour lashings of freshly-picked strawberries mashed with bananas, even though they sometimes made her sick.

Once she fell asleep, and fell off, while they were riding. Tiger went on pedalling for nearly a mile before he discovered that Sybil was no longer with him. He pedalled frantically back to find her weeping by the roadside. But it was with laughter. Her wide-brimmed straw hat had broken her fall and she was quite unhurt.

The inevitable day came (and with it an alternative explanation of Sybil's sickness) when she told Tiger she was going to have a baby. Both knew it meant saying good-bye to the tandem and the open road at week-ends. But it also meant that Tiger must look for another job—he could not possibly support a wife and child on the £4 a week Lewis Waller paid him. It was hard enough on £6. 10s. which was what they earned between them. And when the run of *The White Man* ended, there would be nothing at all.

'I'll have to go abroad again,' he told Sybil finally.

'Can I come too?' she asked.

'Of course, darling, when I've got settled,' Tiger told her.

'Where shall we go?' was her next question.

They ran through the gamut of possibilities from Australia to Zanzibar and finally narrowed the field down to South Africa and South America. Unable to make up their minds, they decided to toss: Heads, South America: tails, South Africa.

Sybil provided the penny. Tiger tossed.

'IT's heads,' Sybil said.

Tiger was sorry in a way. He had loved the smell of the veld—the mimosa, the naked hills after a storm, the vast solitary distances and the incredibly bright stars. And it would have been nice to make friends with the men he had met—and admired—as enemies.

All the same, South America would be an entirely new experience. He adored new experiences.

'I just can't wait till you send me a cable to join you,' Sybil said.

Tiger worked his passage to Buenos Aires in a coal freighter called *Sola* which leaked. She sank in mid-Atlantic not long afterwards.

The *Sola* was near the Equator, a thousand miles from land, when her engines stopped. Inspection showed that the log-line had snapped and the captain inferred that it had got mixed up with the propeller when a heavy sea had lifted the boat's stern out of the water. The log was attached to the *Sola*'s stern, not over the side as is the usual practice nowadays.

The *Sola* carried no diving gear, so if they were to free the propeller someone would have to take a very deep breath indeed and dive down with a knife in his hand—and his heart in his mouth, because of sharks. The alternative was to abandon ship and take to the boats unless some other vessel happened to come in sight which was an extremely unlikely chance in those pre-wireless days.

Captain Burns mustered the crew and asked for volunteers. Tiger stepped forward.

He was the only one who could swim.

A boat was lowered and Tiger, clad in an eyelgass and a knife which was tied to his wrist, dived into the water while Captain Burns on deck kept anxious watch for sharks and the men in the boat stood by with boathooks in case one of the brutes attacked.

Tiger found the line well and truly tangled round the propeller. There was not the slightest hope of unwinding it—he had to saw it off piece by piece. He has no idea how often he dived. He only knows it took him the whole of a tropical afternoon. The sharks kept their distance and he forgot about them after a while. He has an idea that, as he was being hauled aboard after removing the last strand, somebody lashed out at a dorsal fin which had come within striking distance. But he is not sure.

The *Sola* reached Buenos Aires without further mishap and Tiger made ready to go ashore and look for a job. He had gone on board with two gold sovereigns and a ten shilling piece in his pocket, having left the rest of his money with Sybil. If he could not find a job before he had spent it, he would have to work his passage somewhere else and try again.

When Tiger went to say good-bye before leaving the ship, Captain Burns put a couple of sovereigns into his hand.

'We owe you that, and more,' he said. 'And if you don't find a job at once, you're welcome to doss down in your old bunk till we sail which won't be for at least a fortnight.'

The first news from England Tiger had when he got to the Argentine was that King Edward VII had died on the previous day. So, for once, we can fix the date of his arrival. King Edward VII died on 6th May 1910.

Tiger decided to spend a few hours, and part of his unexpected windfall, trying to get the feel of Buenos Aires before he went job-hunting. What he saw greatly impressed him—the tall, graceful palm trees, the imposing white buildings which looked as if they were scrubbed down every morning, and above all, he adored the haunting smell of coffee. He admired, too, the white suits and black patent leather boots of the men and their unexpected brimmed, black, pork-pie hats.

By the time he was ready to go back to the *Sola* for his free night's lodging, it was beginning to get dark. He was still a long way from the ship when he heard a scream—a high raucous sound that ebbed into an ominous rattle and then ceased. He remembered the gruesome stories Captain Burns had told him about what too often happened in the port area of Buenos Aires after nightfall. Looking round, he saw that it was just the place for dark deeds: no street lamps, no traffic, not even any pedestrians, but dark corners in plenty where men could lie in wait with their sharp *cuchillos* to kill and rob unwary sailors making their way back alone to their ships.

Seeing an up-turned rowing-boat close by, Tiger decided to creep underneath and stay there till morning.

The next few hours were among the most hair-raising he can remember. Weird, ghostly noises frequently punctured the darkness. More screams, and the yelling of fighting, drunken men, alternated with sinister splashes in the lapping water. He could not sleep but crouched under the sheltering boat, alert and thoroughly cramped, till it began to get light.

He spent several days, but no more nights, tramping to and from the *Sola* and about the city looking for suitable work. Then the Editor of an English-language newspaper which Tiger thinks was the *Standard* advised him to go and see the engineer in charge of the construction work on the Midland Railway, whose name was Solly.

Solly stared at Tiger for a moment and then asked him if he could drive a car. When Tiger said he could, Solly replied:

'Fine. In that case, you may be just the man I'm looking for.'

The job he offered Tiger was to take charge of a section of the line at one end of which was an unfinished bridge. He was to control some eight hundred peons who were building the bridge and also patrol his section of the finished line to make sure it was in working order. This he would have to do on a trolley fitted with an internal combustion engine which was why Solly wanted to know if he could drive a car.

'What happens if I meet a train?' Tiger asked.

'You and your assistant trundle the trolley off the permanent way as quick as you can,' Solly explained. 'Incidentally, the thing weighs nearly a ton but you'll find it quite easy when you get the knack. And, normally, you don't have to hurry—the pampas are dead level and there are no curves for more hundreds of miles than you need bother about. So you can see for miles.'

Then he added, by way of after-thought: 'No, you won't have to worry about the trolley.'

Tiger felt he should leave it to Solly to explain what he did have to worry about and asked where he would live. Solly replied that the company provided a caravan on rails consisting of a kitchen and three rooms each about twelve feet long.

'That's fine,' Tiger said. 'Then I shall be able to bring my wife out.'

'You're married, are you?' Solly asked.

'Yes,' Tiger told him. 'She stayed at home to have her baby—our first, actually. She wants to come out as soon as possible afterwards.'

'If I were you, I'd let her stay where she is,' Solly advised.

'But, why?' Tiger wanted to know. 'She's absolutely set on coming out. Besides, I want her to.'

'Listen,' Solly said. 'The reason there's a vacancy is that those peons I want you to take charge of poured a can of paraffin over your predecessor and set fire to it. He died. Then, there's not another Englishwoman within a hundred miles. There is one Frenchwoman but she will be leaving before long. And, just under where your headquarters will be there's a *belichi* which is a sort of general store where the peons shop and so do the gauchos—they're cowboys. You'll have to shop there, too, by the way. It sells everything, including liquor. Including liquor,' he repeated. 'And there's about as much respect for human life as in the American Wild West.'

'I think I can cope,' Tiger remarked.

'So do I,' Solly agreed. 'That's why I'm going to offer you the job. But I'm worried about your wife. Of course she's young. Is she pretty, too?'

'Very,' Tiger replied.

'Well, there's one thing I haven't mentioned yet,' Solly went on. 'Normally, you'll be away from the caravan the whole of every day. Anything up to a hundred and fifty miles. And that *belichi* is within a hundred and fifty yards of your caravan.'

'We'll be all right,' Tiger assured him.

'I certainly hope so,' Solly replied. 'And in the circumstances, the only thing I can do is to see you have a reliable servant. It so happens I can put you on to one at once. His name is Nicolas Adolfini and his home is only a few miles from where I propose to send you.'

The place was called Carhuie and Tiger arrived there a few days later with the caravan, weighing eighty tons, coupled to his trolley. With him were his assistant, who was a peon, and Nicolas Adolfini. With him also were a revolver and his swordstick. He soon added a short-handled hatchet which he took with him wherever he went, leaving the revolver with Sybil.

There were two lengths of siding at Carhuie and Tiger backed his caravan on to one of them. The other was occupied by an engineer named Waters whose French wife had a tame sparrow she had brought from Colombo. The Waters, as Solly had predicted, left soon after Sybil arrived.

Just beyond Tiger's siding was a drop of some twenty feet in which lay a heterogeneous pile of firewood. Some sixty to seventy yards beyond the drop was the *belichi*. Every evening, the railway peons, and gauchos from the surrounding country, gathered there to drink, gamble, play cards—and fight. The favourite gambling game was one in which a man spread his fingers apart on the table and then moved them swiftly while he stabbed at the spaces between with the point of his *cuchillo*. If he cut a finger, he paid, if he avoided them successfully, the other man paid. After a while, the roles were exchanged.

The din from the *belichi* went on far into the night except on Saturday nights when it continued till the Sunday evening. There were frequent brawls, and duels in which the combatants wrapped their gaily-coloured ponchos round their left arms so that they could ward off or catch the blows their adversaries aimed at them with their deadly *cuchillos*. Sometimes a man incautiously got himself killed, in which case his relatives or friends generally killed the killer.

Tiger kept clear of the *belichi* and, when he needed anything, he sent Adolfini to buy it. Adolfini worked for Tiger, and later for Sybil, from dawn to dusk. Then he mounted a horse and rode away to his home—where that was Tiger never knew.

Sybil remembers Adolfini as a good cook spoiled by a passion for olive oil. He used olive oil for everything except making tea which was not the tea we know, but the so-called *maté* which Sybil found quite palatable when she got used to it. Everything was very cheap. Beef and mutton cost about a penny a pound. Green vegetables and potatoes were unobtainable. But there was plenty of rather coarse spaghetti and also of far-too-hard, horrible, tasteless, biscuit-like bread.

Solly had not exaggerated when he warned Tiger he would generally be out all day. When he had not returned by nightfall, Sybil used to lock the door of the caravan and watch for the reflection of the head-lights of the trolley in the sky—visible for as much as thirty-five to forty miles across the flat, endless pampas. As soon as she saw them, she used to start to get their supper ready—she knew he would normally be back in about an hour.

A night came, however, when a herd of wild horses charged at the trolley. They did not actually touch it but stood snorting and squealing just in front of it. It took nearly an hour to edge past them. Then, about ten miles from Carhuie, they ran slap into a herd of cattle asleep on the line. The trolley was a casualty as well as one of the cattle so Tiger left his assistant to spend the night with the trolley and set off on foot to reassure Sybil.

'I'm so glad you're all right,' she said when he arrived. 'What happened?'

He told her and then, noticing that she seemed worried, asked what was the matter.

'Nothing, really,' she told him. 'I heard someone prowling round, about an hour ago. But when I went to the door and called out: "Is that you, Tiger?" he went away.'

'I expect he came because the trolley isn't in its usual place, so he thought I was away for the night,' Tiger surmised. 'I don't suppose it'll happen again. But if it should, don't hesitate to use the revolver if he tries to make trouble.'

'I'm certain I should miss,' Sybil confessed. 'Besides, it's in Buenos Aires being mended. Don't you remember?'

'So it is,' Tiger agreed. 'I had forgotten.'

As soon as Tiger had had something to eat, they went to bed. Tiger was already asleep when Sybil nudged him gently and whispered:

'Ssh! The man's back again. He put his arm through the window and started fingering me. When I moved without speaking, he took his arm away. What shall I do if he comes back?'

'He won't,' Tiger said, immediately slipping out of bed.

He went outside and soon saw a foot protruding from underneath the caravan, so he caught hold of it and pulled. The peon managed to kick himself free and leaped at Tiger with his *cuchillo*. But his slash went wide and, before he could recover, Tiger's fist caught him on the jaw. The man crashed down on to the firewood the long nails of which went right through his clothes and embedded themselves in his back.

Tiger says he is quite certain that the man impaled himself on nails protruding from a sleeper and that he lay there screaming, unable to move, till his fellow-peons interrupted their carousing at the *belichi* and came to free him. Sybil is equally certain that she was helpless with hysterical laughter at seeing him run along the railway track with a plank about six feet long firmly attached to his backside and waggling from side to side with each step.

I must confess I like Sybil's version best. It gives the poor devil his exact due, namely, about four inches apiece of doubtless rusty nails embedded deeply enough in his posterior to make him quite sure the devil himself was on his tail.

But poetic justice is not always achieved so it may be that Tiger's version is correct though they must have been some nails to have emerged far enough on the farther side of a sleeper for a man to impale himself on. So I shall maintain a somewhat partial neutrality and merely take the opportunity to point out how tricksy memory can be over points of detail.

Tiger liked the pampas with their waving alfalfa and huge cacti and almost complete absence of trees. Sybil found the climate too hot and the loneliness got on her nerves. The fear of unexpected dangers she might have to face was with her throughout the day and night.

Once she saw a furry thing on the ground that looked so attractive she bent down to stroke it. Then it moved and she saw it was a spider—big enough to cover the whole palm of her hand. She screamed and Tiger came and put his foot on it. I think it was probably harmless, not a tarantula. But it was horrible whatever it was.

Every now and then there were tremendous storms. Some were preceded by hordes of insects—including spiders, but little ones—and what Tiger says were red, flying centipedes and Sybil brown flying ants. Whatever they were they covered the floor of the caravan to a depth of several inches before she and Tiger could get the door and windows shut. And there they stayed crawling and writhing till the rain came and Sybil could sweep the intruders out.

One day, the sky grew pitch dark and they thought a storm was coming. Then there was a rushing sound as of wind but no thunder and no rain except a rain of locusts. Very soon the insects lay in drifts ten feet deep and even more. And as the broiling sun beat down on them there was an insufferable smell of oily fish.

It happened that Tiger had not gone out to inspect the line that morning. Later, when he started up the trolley's engine, the wheels could not bite and he was unable to leave the siding either that day or the next. On the third morning, all the locusts had disappeared, except the casualties. And every green thing on the whole face of the pampas had disappeared with them.

Another day, during a real thunderstorm when the rain was like a flowing wall, a thing that Sybil calls a thunderbolt, fell just in front of the caravan. It was still quite warm when Tiger dug it out of the ground—a jagged, irregular piece of metal about four inches long, three across and two thick. From its appearance, it seems to have been a meteorite but, if so, as Sybil reasonably asks, why did it choose to fall during a thunderstorm? She says she has never heard of one falling out of a clear sky. And neither have I.

Sybil stuck it at Carhuie until her son fell ill with what was called locally 'sandwater fever' which is some kind of bladder trouble. The nearest doctor lived on the far side of the bridge which was still unfinished. But they had to get the child across somehow.

The rails were in position, but not enough of the sleepers to make it possible to walk over the bridge while carrying a baby. The engineer in charge said he thought the structure would bear the weight of the trolley though he could not guarantee it.

They got across safely and back again with the whole structure swaying and groaning, and the child recovered.

Before arrangements could be made for Sybil to take him

back to England, trouble of a different kind arose. The peons got out of control and rushed threateningly at Tiger. He had his hatchet in his hand and there was nothing he could do but use it. The man he hit fell dead with his head in two pieces and the other rioters fled hastily lest the '*loco Inglez*', mad Englishman, should cleave their heads open too.

Before Sybil left, she gave the child's cot to Adolfini. She had brought it from England and there was not another like it in the country, so he was delighted. On their way to Buenos Aires a few days later, they were crossing a river—a different one, with a proper railway track—when Sybil clutched Tiger's arm.

'Look,' she said. 'There's our cot.'

It was sailing majestically along in mid-stream all by itself with a baby in it. They never heard what happened to it. The floods that year were the worst the Argentine had known for a generation, sweeping away whole villages, not merely the cot and poor Adolfini's baby.

Tiger saw Sybil and their son safely on board the boat which took them back to England and then went to ask Solly to find him another job. He could earn much more in the Argentine than he could in England—and Sybil was already going to have another baby.

Solly offered him a post as tally clerk on some levelling work at the railway terminus.

'There's been some hanky-panky down at the site,' he told Tiger. 'Will you try to sort it out?'

'Certainly,' Tiger said. 'Tell me about it.'

THE tally clerk from whom Tiger took over was a German, named Heinrich Schlachter, a rather dreamy, retiring, helpless little man whom Solly had sacked because tallies were being presented for payment in respect of cartloads of soil allegedly delivered on the site but never actually received.

'Heinrich swears he's not responsible,' Solly explained. 'But, when I asked him if he suspected anybody, he told me he would rather not say. So I was obliged to assume he is doing the fiddle himself. And he quite possibly isn't.'

'You're sure there is a fiddle?' Tiger asked.

'Absolutely,' Solly replied. 'I've had a chap keeping count down at the site. Last week we were charged for a hundred and fifty-eight cartloads of soil and we only received ninety-eight.

The man responsible for bringing the soil was also a German, a hefty fellow to whom Tiger took an immediate dislike. But he could not detect any irregularity until one day he came back to his office and found the German rummaging among the papers in his desk.

'You mustn't do that,' Tiger said sharply.

'Why not?' the other asked. 'You weren't here and I needed some of those tallies.'

'When you want them, you ask me,' Tiger declared. 'I'm in charge of them, not you.'

'I can't ask you if you're not here,' the German pointed out.

'If I'm not here,' Tiger told him, 'you must wait till I come back.'

The German laughed.

'Come off it,' he remarked, still laughing. 'Why not sign the whole lot and pass them over to me so I can hand them in as I deliver the loads? It'll save you a hell of a lot of trouble.'

He paused a moment and then added:

'And when I say trouble, I mean—trouble.'

'I see,' Tiger remarked with a glint in his one eye. 'And supposing I don't want to save—trouble.'

'Then you'll get plenty,' the other promised. 'Think it over.'

After the man had gone, Tiger counted the tallies and came to the conclusion that a good many were missing though he could not absolutely swear to it. So he arranged that every tally he handed out would bear an inconspicuous secret mark on the back.

Two or three days later, Solly came round to Tiger's office and said:

'That German driver put in two tallies too many yesterday and three today. But what are we going to do? He isn't our employee, so I can't sack him. And if I report him, his firm will say it's none of their business. Which, of course, it isn't.'

'Leave him to me,' Tiger suggested.

'Take care,' Solly warned. 'He's an ugly-looking customer. We don't want you with a knife in your ribs.'

Tiger laughed. 'You needn't worry,' he said. 'I'll be all right. I'm not so sure about him.'

More unmarked tallies turned up on the following days and the next time Tiger saw the German, he called across the yard:

'Come here! I want to talk to you.'

'All right, spit it out,' the German replied, without moving. 'I'm not deaf.'

'If you want everybody to hear me call you a thief, I will,' Tiger said. 'Last week you presented a hundred and twenty tallies for payment. I only issued ninety-six. You stole the others.'

'You're a liar,' the German blustered. 'As well as a fool.'

He walked over to where Tiger was standing and shook his fist in his face.

'I said you're a liar,' he repeated. 'But supposing I did pinch a few of those bloody tallies, how d'you propose to prove it? And what do you propose to do about it? Peach on me? If you did, you might find yourself at the bottom of the harbour with a piece of rock tied round your neck.'

'All the tallies I issued were marked,' Tiger told him. 'Twenty-four of those you presented weren't. Here they are in case you would like to see them before I tear them up. As for your threats, I'm not that poor little devil, Heinrich. And I don't stand for being called a liar.'

'Oh, you don't, don't you?' the German remarked, lunging out at Tiger.

He missed. Tiger's right caught him on the jaw as he lurched forward and the German crumpled up on the floor, groaning.

Tiger hauled him to his feet and shook him.

'Now, listen, you dirty rat,' he said. 'If you ever show your face here again, I'll hit you hard enough to break your jaw. I shan't talk. I shall just hit. So clear out. And get another job.'

He repeated: 'Get another job.'

Whether the man took the hint or took too long over planning his revenge, Tiger never saw him again. He himself left Buenos Aires a few weeks later. A revolution had broken out in Mexico and he felt it offered him a golden opportunity not only for a little excitement but for a job. After all, he was an experienced soldier.

So he left Buenos Aires in the autumn of 1911, which of course is our spring, *en route* for Veracruz.

Tiger stated quite frankly in an article published in the *People's Journal*, Dundee, on 7th March 1914 that, when he went to Mexico he had very little idea of what the Mexicans were fighting about. He said he really went there 'for the fun of it'.

Presumably, therefore, he offered his services to the rebel leader, Francisco Madero on the broad ground that Governments are usually in the wrong. Madero made him tactical adviser to a force of fifteen thousand operating in the State of Chihuahua. The men were seething with discontent, mainly because they had not been paid for several months.

The obvious remedy was to get funds by raiding a bank. Having broken in, they blew the safe open with a charge of dynamite. They destroyed its contents while doing so. The net proceeds of the operation were worth, in English money, about fourpence.

Moving over towards the Pacific coast, the rebels, and Tiger, laid siege to the town of Guadelajara which soon decided to capitulate. But no one could be found to risk handing over the keys to the rebels until the British Consul, Grenville Holmes, offered to make the formal act of surrender on behalf of the civic authorities.

He marched unconcernedly out to meet the rebel commander through a regular forest of menacing machine guns with his pipe, not his heart, in his mouth. He was not a little surprised when he found that the rebel commander had deputed another Englishman to receive him—and the keys.

If Holmes, as the official representative of the British Government to the Mexican Government, felt any embarrassment at having to deal with an Englishman acting on behalf of the rebels, he certainly did not show it. Indeed, he invited Tiger to dinner. I suppose the civic authorities must have paid a handsome sum into the rebel exchequer for there was very little looting so that Tiger and Holmes were able to see quite a lot of one another during the next few days.

It was twenty-five years before they met again. Tiger was flat-hunting in Balham and was talking to the wife of the man who was in charge of the block of flats he was inspecting. She told him she was Hawaiian and mentioned that she had met her husband in Mexico. When Tiger said he knew parts of Mexico well, she said, 'You must come and meet my husband, ah, there he is!'

The two men shook hands, then looked at one another and finally burst out laughing.

Tiger soon discovered that the Mexican revolution was not such fun as he had expected. One day, as he was riding across an open space with his men, he saw a pole with something tied to it which was swarming with ants. Looking closer, he realized that the 'something' had once been a human being. Either the rebels or the Government's troops had tied a living man to the pole and spread a trail of honey from him to a nearby ants' nest. The man had been eaten alive.

Some time later, Tiger saw a human body which had been pegged down on top of a plant with spear-like leaves. They had grown right through the flesh and were pushing upwards through the man's chest and stomach. Tiger hopes the poor devil died of thirst before the spikes penetrated into a vital organ. But the plant grew very fast.

Though Tiger found Mexican methods of dealing with their

enemies utterly revolting, he liked the people. In 1927, he went there again when the country was at peace and thoroughly enjoyed himself as we shall see.

But in 1911, Mexico offered him no solution to his immediate problem which was to make enough money to ensure that his wife had her second baby in comfort. So we very soon find him on his way back to London where he put on his silk hat with the usual accessories, picked up his gold-knobbed cane to increase the appearance of affluence and went out to look for a job.

A few days later, the Warwick Film Company in the Charing Cross Road offered to train him as a cameraman. The starting pay was £2 a week to be raised to £4 if he gave satisfaction.

He appears to have done so for, in quite a short while, we find him sitting on a sort of trapeze under the Willow Airship waiting to be filmed, and to film himself, as he floated down to earth with the help of a parachute—a real one, not his father's umbrella.

14. 'SHOOTING' A BALKAN WAR

TIGER got on to his trapeze before the airship left her moorings at Hendon and sat there swaying while the airship climbed and then made its way over Hampstead Heath. His movie camera was a new type invented by a dimunitive Pole named Pryzinski. It was operated by compressed air and strapped to his waist. He and it weighed between them over three hundredweight. A colleague in the airship stood by to film him taking off: another was waiting below in a fast car to shoot the landing. Tiger himself was to film anything that took his fancy.

The actual moment of take-off was decided by the commander of the airship. Tiger had simply to sit on his trapeze beneath the vessel's nose till he saw her floating away from him, when he was to start pushing the button which controlled the compressed air. In most cameras of those days there was no button to press and, unless the operator wound at a constant speed, the resulting pictures were as jumpy as a flea circus.

On reflection, I think 'take-off' may not be the correct word. What actually happened was that when the airship's commander judged that he had reached the right spot and elevation, he suddenly and without warning disconnected the trapeze thus precipitating Tiger into space.

The result of, so to say, jettisoning three hundredweight of ballast from the nose of the airship was that the nose in question shot straight up and Tiger's colleague slid straight down the whole length of the deck dropping his camera which went overboard without benefit of parachute.

Meanwhile, Tiger himself was pointing nose downwards with nothing to point his camera at except Hampstead Heath which was approaching at considerable speed. By the time he had got his legs where they ought to be, the parachute had started spinning like a top. So had Tiger. And by the time he had finally decided that there was nothing he could do about it, he realized that in a matter of moments the trolley-bus lines at Golder's Green would do it for him. He wondered vaguely whether his colleague in the car would arrive from Hampstead Heath in time to film them doing so; also what it felt like to be electrocuted.

Then the wind changed and Tiger found himself being mysteriously wafted upwards, still spinning, in the direction of Hendon. The wind finally spun him into the middle of the Welsh Harp. There was no water in it, only mud. At least Tiger thought it was only mud till he put a foot through a bicycle wheel and a hand on to a decaying cat. As he struggled to stand up, he entangled himself in a bedstead and the parachute clung lovingly round his head and shoulders.

I wonder if he thought of the pretty housemaid, Fatty, displaying her unmentionables in a welter of printer's varnish.

Onlookers rescued him in the end with the help of ladders and planks. His camera which was strapped round his middle was coated with the Welsh Harp mud. The camera in the fast car had lost all track of Tiger even before the wind changed. So the net result of the exercise from the Warwick Film Company's standpoint was one camera to the bad and no pictures.

Filming any kind of news story in those days was apt to be an adventure. Apart from the difficulty of handling and winding the cameras, there was fierce competition between the various newsreel companies and even between the newsreels and evening papers.

On every importa.... occasion, the cameraman was surrounded by a posse of 'protectors' to see that a rival company did not ditch his camera. Whoever took rolls of films to the car which was waiting to rush them to London, also had to be protected on his way to the car. So did the car on its way to London. But, if the protection really did protect, the newsreel companies actually got their pictures to the cinemas before the evening papers came out with more than the bare news.

Operating the camera—keeping the speed steady and the lens correctly pointed—gave the operators so much to do that they often had no time to watch what they were filming. They just went on turning the handle till there was nothing more to film, or till they had used all the film.

The year Tiger filmed the Derby—or part of it—was a historic one. As he rushed into the office, the Editor flashed at him:

'Well, have you got it?'

'Got what?' Tiger asked.

'That suffragette throwing herself under the horses, you fool,' the Editor snorted. 'And getting killed.'

'Oh, that,' Tiger replied. 'Of course.'

'Then why didn't you say so?' the Editor snapped.

Actually, all Tiger had seen and heard was a flurry of horses. As soon as the beat of their hooves ended, he dismantled his camera as fast as he could and hurried to the car which was waiting for him. He had no idea that there had been a tragedy.

But his luck was in. He had filmed it without having seen it.

The months passed and war-clouds began to gather in the Balkans. Tiger was now working for Pathé Gazette and managed to convince his employers that the clouds really were going to break. So he arrived in Constantinople (which is now Istanbul) several weeks before the war started. The local man who represented Pathé, France, ordered him (unsuccessfully) to clear out. But it was not long before Pathé had no less than eight expert staff correspondents dealing with the war, some on the Bulgarian side, some on the Turkish. But Tiger seems to have been the only one at the front with the Turkish Army.

As usual, he managed to mix himself up with the fighting. In the *Bioscope* of 5th December 1912, there is a picture of Tiger in camp at Chorlu and a caption underneath it saying that his 'magnificent pictures of the war have caused so much sensation.'

The *Bioscope* then goes on to quote extracts from his letters and cables. 'I have been smashed up once or twice,' he says. 'I have just been five days in the saddle and present during the last five days at the most murderous fighting on the right flank.' 'Very difficult getting pictures, no correspondents allowed at front, having to dodge. Cannot get servants stay with me, run away when shelled. Camera body draws enemy fire, mistaken for maxim . . . only four correspondents at front all time, rest in Constantinople.'

I don't think Tiger was correct in saying that all the correspondents except four stayed in Constantinople, though it was probably a better place from which to get a general picture of what was happening than anywhere else. But Tiger himself was not there often, so it was quite impossible for him to say where any correspondent was unless he was where Tiger was.

There appear to have been at least one hundred and fifty newspapermen altogether in Turkey: American, French, German and many other nationalities besides British. They included Colonel Lionel James of *The Times*, Francis McCullough of the *Daily News*, Angus Hamilton of the *Central News*, Zeppings Wright of the *Illustrated London News* and Hubert Wilkins (afterwards Sir Hubert and a famous explorer), who was at first Tiger's deadliest rival because he represented Gaumont, and was soon to become his very dear friend.

Zeppings Wright was an elderly man with a beard who arrived at the Toketlian Hotel (where Tiger was staying at a cost of six pounds a day) carrying a white enamel chamber-pot under his arm. He explained that he suffered from dysentery and did not wish to be caught unawares.

Not being well enough to go to the front, Zeppings Wright made his drawings from descriptions given him by his colleagues. After the battle of Luleburgaz at which the Turks were defeated, Tiger described to him the capture of a sugarloaf hill which decided the day in favour of the Bulgars. Zeppings Wright only asked a few questions but when he showed his drawing to Tiger it was correct in almost every detail.

Some of the correspondents were obliged to stay in Constantinople by a Turkish Government order that each must have six months' provisions with him, three mules and not less than four hundred pounds in gold. Most of the mules had already been commandeered by the Turkish authorities and Tiger seems to have made a corner in the rest on behalf of Pathé Gazette. Those he did not need he presented to the Turkish Government. I doubt if his action was popular with the other correspondents.

Another snag which confronted one and all was someone to whom Tiger referred in his letters published in the *Bioscope* as 'the *dear old lady* who *nurses* correspondents'. 'Her' correct name was Wasfy Bey to whom the Turkish High Command had deputed the quite impossible task of keeping one hundred and fifty newspapermen out of trouble, out of mischief and in touch both with events and the censor at one and the same time.

When the battle of Luleburgaz was in progress, at least three correspondents evaded Wasfy Bey's clutches unknown to each other. They were Wilkins, Francis McCullough and Tiger himself.

Tiger's servant happened to be holding his own and his master's horses when a shell exploded about half a mile away. He immediately dropped both reins and fled on foot, followed (according to some verses Tiger subsequently perpetrated in honour of Hubert Wilkins) by a shot from Tiger's revolver to speed the man's return to Constantinople by taking the skin off his backside. Fortunately Tiger's aim seems to have been accurate.

Tiger caught his own horse, an Arab with the descriptive name of Eclair, but failed to catch his servant's which was carrying a week's supply of food. As he jogged on disconsolately, he saw two horsemen on ahead apparently engaged in a tug-of-war. One of the reins snapped and a moment later a horse and rider were galloping madly towards Tiger.

The rider was Wilkins's servant. Tiger covered him with his revolver and ordered him to stop. When Wilkins arrived, he and Tiger decided to send the servant packing and team up together instead of competing—it was obviously impossible to set up a camera, take pictures and hold a horse at the same time. So they agreed to take it in turns which should do which. From then on, they always took the same pictures when they were together, which was most of the time though not always. Whatever their employers thought, there was nothing they could do about it.

As Wilkins and Tiger were riding off with their one led horse to get closer to the fighting, a third correspondent joined them. It was Francis McCullough.

Afterwards, they rode back together to Constantinople to send off their material without the censor seeing it.

On another occasion, Tiger was with Angus Hamilton when they saw horsemen on a hill in front of them.

Tiger looked at them through his field glasses and told Hamilton that they were Bulgars.

'Nonsense,' Hamilton replied. 'But, even if they are, what does it matter? We're non-combatants.'

Tiger was as sure the horsemen were Bulgars as he was that the word 'non-combatant' meant nothing at all. He tried to convince Hamilton, but failed. So he said he was going; and went.

Hamilton was taken prisoner and horribly mutilated with bayonets. He recovered but committed suicide in New York some time afterwards.

Once Tiger himself fell into the hands of bandits who were operating in no-man's-land. After they had taken the contents of his pockets, and the food on his spare horse, the bandit chief started to examine first his cine-camera and then his films—by the light of two candles.

The more Tiger tried to dissuade him, the more certain the bandit chief was that the films were valuable. He was a tallish man with a heavy beard and as he unrolled foot after foot of film and could see nothing on it, he bent his head nearer to the light to make sure he was not missing anything.

Suddenly there was a bright flash and when the smoke cleared, the film had disappeared. So had the tent, the bandit's beard, hair and eyebrows, and most of his clothes. He was also very sore in more senses than one.

'Take him away,' he yelled to his followers and shaking his fist as he lay prostrate on the floor. 'Make him dig his grave. Then shoot him. When you have filled the grave in, come and tell me.'

The bandits hustled Tiger out, put a long-handled, pointed spade into his hands and then sat around to watch him dig.

'Do any of you speak English?' he asked after a while. And when no one answered, he added: 'I might be able to make it worth your while.'

One of the men grinned and said he understood a little. However, it proved to be enough to arrange that he should go and fetch Tiger's camera and then accompany him to Constantinople to collect a further £400 in gold. Meanwhile the other bandits were to fire a volley over the 'grave', fill it in and then return to tell their charred chief that his order had been carried out.

During the Turkish retreat past Chorlu to Chatalja, a Turkish soldier came up to him and asked for a drink of water. The man was clasping his stomach with both hands and, when Tiger looked to see why, he realized that the man's entrails were actually oozing out through a deep gash which had presumably been made by a bayonet. The man had plastered mud over the wound to help hold his stomach together and had set out on foot with his comrades and with his hands pressed against the mud. When Tiger met him, he must have already walked about twenty-five miles.

Tiger made him lie down, gave him a drink of water and bandaged the gaping wound as best he could, after which the Turk insisted on being helped to his feet. Tiger watched him stagger on down the road which was cluttered with the remnants of the defeated Turkish Army and wondered how far he would get before he dropped down and died.

About a fortnight later in Constantinople, he was talking to a Turkish doctor who said:

'Do you know, I've a man in my hospital who came in about a week ago with half his inside in his hands. Actually, *in* his hands. His intestines had come out through a great gash in the wall of his stomach and if he had not clasped his hands underneath them they would have fallen to the ground. Why he was not dead, I simply do not know, but the extraordinary thing is that he is going to recover. He says he walked all the way from Luleburgaz but, of course, that's utterly impossible. It's a good hundred miles.'

'I agree it's impossible,' Tiger replied. 'But I happen to know it's true. I gave him a drink of water myself and tried to bandage him up near Chorlu. I thought of putting him on my horse but he would have fallen off if I had. I thought he would prefer to die on his feet. I never dreamed he would get beyond half a mile.'

Tiger attributes the defeat of the Turks in the first Balkan War to corrupt contractors and corrupt or inept politicians who sent some of the bravest soldiers in the world to their death by supplying cardboard bullets, shells that did not explode and guns which burst when they were fired. He was delighted when their enemies fell out over the spoils and gave the Turks a chance to re-occupy Adrianople and recover part of their losses.

He came home in 1913 and was 'axed' by Pathé soon afterwards—when the war ended they needed fewer cameramen.

But he still went on filming. He spent some time with the celebrated Punch artist, Harry Furness, making a film on the sea-front at Eastbourne. The heroine was a girl named Peggy, aged about twelve. Tiger hadn't the slightest idea what the story was, and he suspects Furness hadn't either. But when Tiger expostulated at shooting the same scene over and over again at 2/- a foot, Furness went purple in the face and told him to keep his mouth shut which Tiger did in future.

Another film assignment, probably for the Williamson Film Company, was to take pictures of Sir Hiram Maxim's tests of a new armour-piercing rifle bullet. Tiger stood in an alcove near the target with his camera and Sir Hiram was to fire his machine gun down a corridor measuring perhaps twenty-five yards.

Unfortunately there had been a mistake and the bullets fired were soft-nosed ones which, instead of piercing the target, bounced back into Tiger's alcove, searing him like a hot soldering iron. As soon as Sir Hiram finished his first burst of fire, Tiger yelled at him not to fire another but Sir Hiram was deaf or just did not hear. Tiger did not dare put his head out to explain in case Sir Hiram started another burst. After enduring several more bombardments, Tiger hit on the idea of pushing his camera into the corridor instead of his head. Sir Hiram then came to see what the trouble was and the experiment came to an end. So, I fear, did the life of the camera.

Tiger's career as a kind of film jack-of-odd-jobs came to an end soon after an Austrian Archduke was killed in the Balkans in 1914.

This time, the flames of war engulfed the world. And when Harold Nicolson woke up the German Ambassador to tell him that Great Britain and Germany were at war, Tiger had already managed to get mixed up in the conflagration.

15. RESISTANCE IN BELGIUM

WHEN Tiger went to offer his services to the War Office shortly before World War I started, his reception was precisely the same as Sir Howard Vincent's at the beginning of the Boer War in 1899.

'Even if there is a war,' Tiger was told, 'we've got seventy thousand men—quite enough to settle the Kaiser's hash. But, you'll see: he's only bluffing. He won't attack Belgium when he realizes we'll be there as soon as he is.'

'What about France?' Tiger inquired. 'And Russia?'

'That's their affair,' the other said. 'We're not bound to help either. Belgium's different. The Kaiser knows that as well as we do. You mark my words: he'll leave Belgium alone.'

'And if he doesn't?' Tiger persisted.

'We'll soon teach him what's what. Good afternoon.'

Tiger reflected that the War Office had been hopelessly wrong in 1899 and would probably prove equally wide of the mark in 1914. But meanwhile, he evidently was not wanted, so he was free to do something else.

He was no longer working for Williamsons who had stopped making newsreels and he decided to try the Transatlantic and Universal Film Company. He told them about his experience in the Balkan Wars, showed them a testimonial from Williamsons which said he was 'thoroughly competent', and asked them to give him a roving commission to film war scenes, and pre-war ones too, in Belgium. They engaged him at once and Tiger arrived in Brussels on 31st July 1914, just before the Germans invaded Belgium.

Although fighting had not actually started, Brussels was jittery with spy mania. As Tiger sat sipping an aperitif outside a café near his hotel, he heard a roar like a pack of angry hyenas and saw a little brown-faced man racing along the street with a huge mob of men and women close behind him. The man was still holding his own when he tripped over the kerb and fell sprawling. The mob was on him before he could get up and it tore him literally to pieces, limb from limb.

Having dealt hideously with one suspected spy, the mob turned to look for others.

'*Regardez-le*,' a man yelled, pointing a bloody finger at Tiger, '*C'est un allemand, bien sûr. Tuez-le. Mort à l'espion.*'

'I'm not a German,' Tiger protested as the mob surged towards him. 'I'm English. Your ally.'

'Liar!' they shouted at him. 'You speak like a German. You must be one with that eyeglass. *A la mort! A la mort!*'

Two gendarmes providentially turned up at this moment. Tiger showed them his passport which they examined and pronounced to be forged. So they pinioned his arms and proceeded to march him off, presumably to the police station, with the mob snarling ominously at their heels.

They had not gone far when Tiger saw an immensely tall, well-dressed man shouldering his way through the throng. When he got close enough, the newcomer shouted to Tiger:

'Say, ain't you British?'

'Of course,' Tiger shouted back. 'I've told these damned fools so and showed them my passport to prove it. They swear it's faked and have taken it away. But it's absolutely genuine. Make them show it you.'

The tall man—he was a good deal taller than Tiger and as thin as a flag-pole—was quite close by this time. He looked curiously at Tiger for a moment and then said:

'Say, chum! Ain't we met before somewhere . . . *Mordieu!*' he went on. 'If it ain't Tiger. Say, what the heck are you doing here. You remember me? Paul J. Selles. You saved my life by Circle City. Up in the Yukon. Or have you forgotten?'

'You really have saved mine,' Tiger declared.

'Wait a moment while I deal with these apes,' Paul said. 'And then we'll go and have a drink.'

The mob had already begun to melt away and it positively wilted when Paul lashed at it in his native tongue. When it had gone, he turned to the gendarmes.

They were entirely unrepentant.

'If we hadn't taken him into custody,' they declared, 'he would be dead by now.'

'Is that why you said his passport was a fake?' Paul asked sarcastically.

'Yes,' they replied. 'We needed an excuse to arrest him. If we had merely looked at his passport, said it was genuine and walked away, the crowd would have worked itself up again and . . . pouf!'

Paul laughed.

'Get along with you,' he told them. 'Come on, Tiger. I need a drink. Several drinks. And I'm sure you do.'

'*Votre passeport, monsieur*,' one of the gendarmes remarked to their retreating backs.

'P'raps he's right,' Paul said to Tiger.

'So you're here to wind that handle,' Paul remarked, pointing at Tiger's cine-camera as he ordered another carafe. 'I thought you might have come to help us fight the bloody Germans.'

'The War Office didn't want me,' Tiger explained.

'I'm not wanted, either,' Paul told him. 'At least, not by the Army. Apparently, my lungs aren't too good. So I'm going to be a *franc-tireur*.'

'What's that?' asked Tiger whose French is not extensive.

'An irregular: a guerilla,' Paul explained. 'Though that's not what the Germans will call us. Like to join us?'

'Would I not,' Tiger exclaimed.

'That's the spirit,' Paul told him. 'It's too late to do anything about it tonight. But tomorrow I'll take you to see Burgomaster Max.'

'Who's he?' Tiger asked.

'Our Lord Mayor,' Paul explained. 'One of the best. A great friend of my father's.'

Paul's father was a professor at Brussels University.

When they went to see Burgomaster Max, they found him seething with indignation. He was as impeccably dressed as Tiger liked to be when in London—frock-coat, a tie-pin and high stiff collar most of which was hidden under a pointed beard.

'We can't possibly hold them,' he told Paul and Tiger. 'All we can hope to do is to delay their advance till the French and British arrive—if the British ever do arrive,' he added looking at Tiger.

'You can count on that,' Tiger assured him.

K   135

'How many?' Burgomaster Max asked.

'Seventy thousand,' Tiger began.

'*Nom d'un nom*,' Burgomaster Max broke in. 'What are seventy thousand? Nothing! They should be a million. But it is not your fault,' he concluded.

'My friend wishes to make it seventy thousand and one,' Paul said with a grin. 'He and I met when I was in Canada. He is an excellent shot. And he's even stronger than I am.'

'Good,' said Burgomaster Max. 'Though strength is not enough. He must be cunning. And ruthless.'

'He'll be both,' Paul promised.

'Do we wear uniform?' Tiger asked.

'No,' Burgomaster Max replied instantly. 'It is *guerre à l'outrance* that we are planning. A national uprising. When the German armies have pushed our soldiers back, the countryside must rise behind them; cut their lines of communication; turn the land into a desert; kill and be killed. The Germans will show no mercy. Nor can we.'

The war was not six hours old before horrible tales of atrocities against the civil population by the German Uhlans began to pour into the Belgian capital. Patrols of Uhlan cavalry it was said, had slipped through the Belgian defences and were looting, murdering, raping, torturing wherever they went.

War always breeds such stories. But what Tiger saw in the days that followed left him in no doubt whatever, that even if the number of atrocities was exaggerated, their ferocity and bestiality out-shamed the worst that invention could devise.

Paul and Tiger went forth with rage in their hearts to kill Uhlans within a few hours of their interview with Burgomaster Max. With them went four others, one of them a girl of about seventeen, the daughter of friends of Paul's parents. Simone had a sawn-off, two-barrelled shot-gun, the men had rifles, three revolvers and a sword-stick. Tiger also had a cine-camera.

It was not long before he came to the conclusion that the cine-camera was in the way. As it did not belong to him, he decided to take it back to London himself. With him went a collection of Uhlan helmets, revolvers, tunics and other trophies which had been amassed by his group of *franctireurs*. Having handed the camera and pictures over to the film company and the trophies to Sybil, he hurried back to Belgium.

He found later that the pictures he had taken were never shown on the screen. They were regarded as too horrible.

Back with Paul, the little band of six scoured the country, hunting and being hunted. Their favourite trick was to reverse the arms of a sign-post and hide close by till a band of Uhlans came and halted to work out which way the sign-post ought to be pointing. If the band was a large one, the *franc-tireurs* did not molest it. But anything under twelve they shot to pieces. Simone preferred not to shoot to kill. She was more concerned with making sure that the Uhlans she shot should never be able to rape again.

Once when Paul and Tiger were sitting unarmed and unconcerned in a country inn, a large car drew up. The driver, who was also the owner, was a civilian and his passengers were three German and two Belgian wounded whom he was taking to hospital. He had stopped because he had run out of petrol.

While he was getting it, a party of Uhlans arrived unexpectedly. Finding three Germans in the car, they seized the driver, stood him up against a wall and shot him. Next they lugged the two wounded Belgians out and shot them too. Then they drove the car off towards the German lines with the three wounded Germans.

The little band of hunters happened to be present when the Germans launched their famous attack on the forts at Namur. The forts looked to Tiger like huge, round mushrooms with machine guns bristling out of their almost-invisible stalks. In front of the mushrooms were rows of pits, each covered with a layer of soil—thick enough to bear the weight of a single man, or even two; thin enough to collapse if a larger number trod on it. The bottom was lined with pointed wooden stakes.

The German infantry came under murderous fire from the mushrooms as they advanced. But they marched on unfalteringly. When the front ranks fell into the pits, the rear ones marched on over their bodies.

Driven back in the end, the Germans brought their artillery into action. The commander of the mushroom in which Tiger was waiting for orders asked him to carry a message to another fort some distance away—Tiger thinks they were numbered respectively four and nine.

He was passing Fort Eight when Fort Nine received a direct hit and disintegrated. Being unable to deliver the message, Tiger carried out the next part of his instructions which were to proceed to the rear and rejoin his little group.

On his way, he passed the Belgian Garde Civile who were waiting for the order to advance and attack the Germans with the bayonet. The men were in civilian clothes and bowler hats. All of them seemed to Tiger to be well over middle age. He never heard what happened to them.

Some time later, Tiger and his group were again sitting in an inn when another Uhlan patrol arrived. Paul had just gone outside and they caught him at once. The innkeeper hid Tiger in a cavity behind a wardrobe. The other four, including Simone, managed to slip away at the back unobserved.

The Uhlans, ranging through the house, barged carelessly against the wardrobe with the result that it came away from the wall. Tiger was unarmed so it was no use trying to resist.

The Uhlans tied his hands together and then his legs and tossed him, like a sack, into a cart. Paul was already there. Next they piled in a plentiful supply of liquor, especially champagne and cognac, harnessed a horse to the cart and drove off.

After perhaps half an hour, they stopped in front of a low wooden building which was presumably a shed about twenty yards long. Paul and Tiger were lifted out of the cart and tossed contemptuously on to a heap of straw where the Uhlans soon forgot about them, partly perhaps because Paul and Tiger, having no wish to be conspicuous, managed to burrow into the straw, but mainly because the Uhlans had more interesting things to occupy their attention.

The ones who had captured Paul and Tiger had drunk freely from the looted bottles as they rode alongside the cart. Those who were already in the hut had evidently been busy in the same way for a considerable time. In fact, Paul and Tiger's arrival interrupted (but not for long) a game of skittles in which bottles of champagne took the place of the pins. Not having a ball, the players used another bottle of champagne instead.

Whenever they managed to knock over (and break) one of the pins, or the 'ball', they raced over the boards on their hands and knees and lapped the champagne off the floor amid gusts of giggly laughter. The Uhlans who had brought Paul and Tiger were fascinated and at once joined in.

Presently the door opened again and an elderly woman in the dress of a nun was brought in. Her captors pulled off her coif, revealing that she had no hair. So one of the Uhlans produced a pencil and made lewd drawings on her head. Then they stripped off her clothes and made similar drawings on her breasts and navel. Finally they raped her and threw her out of the hut.

Their next victim was a girl whom Tiger judged to be about eleven or twelve. When they had undressed her, they threw her down on the floor where one man held her arms and another her legs while a third raped her. Then they changed places. After the first three had finished with her another three took over. Finally they sent her in the wake of the nun and went back to their game of skittles.

The ultimate bestiality was wreaked on three Belgians: a man of about forty, his wife who was about thirty-five and their daughter aged perhaps fifteen. The Uhlans who brought them in evidently thought that the man belonged to the Resistance for as they beat him up they kept on shouting at him to confess who had been 'murdering' German soldiers.

When that had no effect, they asked him if he preferred to watch them extract the information from his wife and daughter.

The woman screamed out: 'Say nothing, Jean. Put your country before us. See the swine in hell before you talk. God will punish them.'

The Uhlans jerked the woman and girl off the ground by their hair and stripped them. Then one of them produced a pair of wire cutters and cut off the woman's nipples before raping her in front of her husband. The girl escaped mutilation but her scalp was bleeding when she was finally thrown on the ground because some of the Uhlans who wanted her pulled her one way by the hair while others tugged at her arms and legs.

Meanwhile, other Uhlans had tied a cord round the man's private parts and were dragging him round the hut.

Finally, all three, still alive, were bundled out through the door and what remained of their clothes was thrown out after them.

Left to themselves, the Uhlans returned to their carousing and they soon began to fall asleep one after the other. In time, the only man still on his feet was a sentry who leant on his rifle just inside the now open door. Even he was far from sober. His head kept dropping forward and it was only this that kept him awake.

Throughout the horrible scenes they had witnessed, Paul and Tiger had been straining at their cords, alternately tensing and flexing their muscles and working to loosen the knots. It was slow work and the daylight had almost gone before Tiger whispered to Paul that his hands were free.

'Don't slip them out of the cord till it's a bit darker,' Paul counselled. 'I'll probably be free too by then. If not, you'll have to untie me.'

'I'm out too,' he whispered a little later. 'Can you get at your feet or shall I?'

'I can manage,' Tiger told him. 'What about you?'

'Same here,' Paul said.

They rubbed their ankles cautiously till the circulation had come back and then Paul told Tiger to wait where he was while he dealt with the sentry. Tiger watched him push the straw aside, almost strand by strand, and inch his way across the floor on his hands and knees. Then Paul was out of sight.

Presently Tiger's straining ears heard a dull thud followed by a gasp and a silence. Soon he saw Paul coming noiselessly towards him, carrying a rifle.

'He won't trouble us,' he observed. 'Come along. We've got to get busy.'

'Did you kill him or just knock him out?' Tiger asked.

'What d'you think?' Paul replied. 'You saw what they did, the bloody swine?'

'What do we do next?' Tiger asked.

'Kill the lot,' Paul told him. 'We can't put them up before a court martial and a firing squad, so we'll simply wring their bloody necks. And then beat it.'

They did exactly that without pity or compunction and

feeling themselves to be the instruments of justice. Then each of them picked up a German rifle and ammunition, put on a German greatcoat and helmet and walked out of the hut.

A German soldier they met wished them good night. Paul, whose German was almost as good as his French—he had been three years at Heidelberg University—answered him and Tiger ventured on a guttural growl in case complete silence should be misunderstood. They strode away into the darkness.

When they had been surprised at the inn, they were making for a farm where Paul was well known. He knew the way and they had nearly reached the place when Tiger suddenly remembered that the Uhlans had taken a valuable telescopic lens from his pocket and that he had seen one of them toss it into a corner of the hut.

'What a fool I was not to look for it,' he remarked as he mentioned his loss casually to Paul.

'Don't worry,' Paul told him. 'I'll go back and get it.'

Tiger told him not to be a fool, but Paul insisted.

'There's not the slightest danger,' he declared. 'I can pass for a German anywhere. Of course, if I see they have already found out what we did, I shall just have to turn round and come back without the lens. If they haven't found out—well I'm not afraid of a few dead bodies. I'll be back in a couple of hours at the outside.'

Acting on Paul's instructions, Tiger knocked at the door of the farm. A girl answered and when he mentioned Paul's name, she pulled him quickly inside and shut the door.

'*Mais où est M. Selles?*' she inquired.

Tiger explained and the girl replied in halting English that he should not have let his friend go. The Uhlans, she said, had been doing dreadful things all day. If Paul was caught, they would torture him. It was madness to have gone back.

Tiger thought so too, especially in view of a certain matter about which the girl as yet knew nothing. But Paul was not a person you could argue with.

The girl went away and came back with a large hunk of bread, a piece of cheese and a bottle of wine.

'Eat these, *monsieur*,' she said. 'And then you must hide. I dare not let you stay in the house. And when M. Selles comes—

if M. Selles comes—he and my father will decide what you are to do next. You cannot stay here. It is much too dangerous.'

She decided that the safest place for him to hide in was a hay-rick which stood at the back of the farmyard, and after Tiger had burrowed into it, the girl piled hay back on top of him. He soon went to sleep.

He was wakened next morning by loud voices and the sound of hammering, doubtless with rifle butts, which came from the direction of the house. He could not see what was happening. He did not need to.

The voices receded as their owners searched the house. Then they grew loud again as the Uhlans came out into the yard.

They clumped up into the loft, banged their way in and out of sheds, some of them came to the hay-rick.

Tiger did not understand what they said. But immediately they had said it, a lance stabbed through the hay just in front of his face. Then another actually went through his sleeve. He could hear the soft swish as other jabs followed to make certain that there was nothing in the rick but hay. Not one of them touched him and presently he heard the Uhlans go away.

It was half an hour before the girl came and called softly:

'Are you all right, *monsieur*.'

'Yes,' he told her. 'What about M. Selles?'

'I think they must have taken him,' she replied. 'But we do not know. When my father goes to the village, he will hear.'

'And they did not molest you?' Tiger asked.

'No,' she said. 'There was an officer with them and he was quite correct. But if they had found you . . .'

She left the sentence unfinished.

'When we know what has happened to my friend, I must go to his help,' Tiger said next.

The girl told him not to be a fool. He could speak no French. He was unmistakable with his monocle. He would be a hindrance to the Belgian patriots, not a help.

Tiger knew she was right and asked her what she advised him to do.

'Wait till my father has been to the village,' she said. 'If M. Selles does not come, we others will send you down to the coast.

You cannot go to Brussels for the Germans are already there. And they are besieging Antwerp. But if you can reach the coast you will be able to rejoin your compatriots.'

The girl's father brought back the news that Paul had certainly been captured and that his friends intended to do their best to rescue him. Meanwhile the other members of Paul's group were making arrangements for Tiger to be taken to the coast after which he must fend for himself.

It is clear from what followed that although World War I had not yet lasted quite three weeks there was already an underground Resistance movement in operation in Belgium and it had even improvised an escape route on lines which paralleled the organization that brought back so many Allied airmen from behind the German lines in World War II.

That night, someone conducted Tiger across fields and along byways to a second hiding place. It was an eerie journey which took almost all night. Frequent flashes and an occasional rumble told of the battle which was in progress away to the south-west. Sometimes, when they came to a main road they had to wait while lines of lorries passed before the guide beckoned to Tiger to rise from their hiding place and make a dash for the other side.

At last they reached a clump of trees and the guide told Tiger to stay there while he went forward to reconnoitre. He came back twenty minutes later with another man who patted Tiger on the shoulder, called him '*mon vieux*' and took him to the kitchen where he was soon tucking in to more bread and cheese and drinking cup after cup of excellent coffee.

He spent the next fifteen hours in a loft eating and sleeping, with nothing but the distant rumble of guns to remind him that he was a fugitive. Soon after nightfall, his host took him to his next refuge and so it went on till one night the guide led him to a culvert, or maybe it was a disused sewer. He does not know where it was nor how many nights it took him to get there. But it appears to have been in the neighbourhood of some fishing village, or holiday resort—possibly Heist.

The culvert, or sewer, ran underground for what seemed an interminable time to Tiger, bent almost double as he stumbled along it. The sun had risen when they came out into the open air and Tiger could see a number of boats drawn up on the sand some distance ahead.

His guide pushed his head up cautiously, took a careful look round and then beckoned Tiger to follow him. As they strode on towards the beach, he suddenly stiffened.

'*Morbleu!*' he said. '*Allemands!*'

He gripped Tiger's arm and pointed to the boats, then turned and ran stealthily back towards the sewer which was less than a hundred yards away. The boats were perhaps three times as far and the Germans, fortunately, more than half a mile.

As Tiger started to run, literally for his life, the Germans saw him and sent a few shots after him but they all went wide. He soon reached the boats and had nearly got one of them into the water when he realized it had no oars. The next one had none, either, nor the next. But he found a pair at last and a minute later he was pulling furiously out to sea.

He was a goodish way from the shore before the Germans reached it and began to take pot shots at him. One bullet splintered an oar and another ripped through the woodwork of the boat but above the waterline. Then the firing stopped. He was out of range. They did not launch another boat and follow him. Tiger believes it was because he had taken the only set of oars.

The weather was calm and Tiger soon decided to row across the Channel instead of along the coast to Calais. For all he knew, the Germans might have already got there.

It was a long and tiring journey, all the more so as he had no food or water. But he says he enjoyed it. He has certainly repeated it on a number of occasions since—not, of course, by the same route and preferably in a canoe.

After a good night's rest, he went back to London, put on his morning coat and went to see Lord Kitchener whose outstretched finger pointed at him from every hoarding on the way and told him he was needed by his country.

Kitchener was godfather to one of Tiger's sons—he had refused to be godfather to a daughter. He heard what Tiger had to say about events behind the German lines in Belgium and then said, casually:

'I suppose you would like a commission.'

KITCHENER told Tiger to report to a cavalry regiment at Tidworth as soon as he had got his uniform, which the military tailor in Jermyn Street undertook to have ready for him in forty-eight hours. His Boer War sword had gone the way most swords seem to go, so he went to Wilkinson's and bought another. Within three days, he was on his way to Tidworth, resplendent in morning coat and top hat with his new uniform, Sam Browne belt and high leather boots packed in a suitcase.

'I have come to report for duty—War Office instructions,' he told the Orderly Room sergeant when he arrived.

'Name, sir?'

'Sarll—T. W. H. Lieutenant. I held a commission during the Boer War,' he added, to explain why he had two pips instead of one.

The sergeant picked up a book and thumbed over a few pages. Then he thumbed them back again.

'Will you wait here a moment, if you please,' he told Tiger. He came back about five minutes later with the adjutant.

'Who are you?' the adjutant asked.

'Lieutenant T. W. H. Sarll, sir. Reporting for duty,' Tiger said.

'Indeed?' the adjutant remarked. 'Well, we have no record of anyone named Sarll being gazetted to us.'

'But Lord Kitchener himself told me to report here,' Tiger began.

'Lord Kitchener?' the adjutant snorted. 'Nonsense! Lord Kitchener is much too busy to concern himself with the appointment of junior officers. I don't believe you.'

'But it's perfectly true, sir,' Tiger insisted. He was going on to say that Kitchener was his second son's godfather but thought better of it. The adjutant might attribute Tiger's two pips to favouritism especially as he could not know that Tiger had previously worn three.

'Is it,' the adjutant said—but not as a question. 'Well, I

think you're a liar. And quite probably a German spy. . . .
Sergeant, have this man put under close arrest.'

Tiger was held incommunicado for two or three days. Then
the adjutant sent for him.

'Your statement that you had been gazetted to this regiment
appears to be correct,' he told Tiger. 'Why you did not bring
the necessary documentary evidence to prove your assertion,
I simply cannot conceive. In the circumstances, you only have
your own stupidity to blame for being held under arrest while
I made inquiries.'

In the mess that evening, Tiger was the only officer in
ordinary service kit and the adjutant ticked him off again.

'The officers of this regiment,' he declared, 'are expected
to wear mess kit in the evenings unless they are on duty. We
do not allow our traditions to go to pot in war time. It would
be bad for morale. I expect you to get mess kit at once.'

'But I can't afford to, sir,' Tiger said.

'Then you should not have joined this regiment,' the
adjutant replied, turning away abruptly.

The next brush came some days later when one of the officers
pooh-poohed a statement in a newspaper that the Germans
were using nineteen-inch guns.

'It's perfectly true,' Tiger declared. 'I've seen them.'

'Where?' they asked.

'Near Namur. About three weeks ago,' Tiger explained.

'What were you doing at Namur three weeks ago?' they
asked next. 'That was when the Germans captured it. You
were a civilian then. Or supposed to be. It sounds very fishy.'

'Actually, I was fighting with the Belgian Resistance,' Tiger
said. 'As a civilian, of course. We were all civilians.'

There was silence for a few moments. Then one of the
officers looked up from the paper he was reading and remarked:

'I say, you chaps, look at this.'

He held up a picture of a collection of German steel helmets
and other trophies in a window of a shop at Southend. Underneath was a caption which said that the trophies had been
brought back from Belgium by Captain T. W. H. Sarll who
had got them while filming scenes at the front for the Trans-

atlantic Newsreel Company. The paper even gave the regiment's name, but I prefer not to do so.

'I suppose you had that put in,' the reader said, pushing the paper under Tiger's nose, 'to get a little free advertisement for yourself, of course.'

'I did nothing of the kind,' Tiger contradicted hotly. 'It's quite true I brought those things back with me. And I did lend them to the shop in Southend to put on show in their window to stimulate recruiting. But that was before I got my commission in this regiment. I never gave them leave to mention my name. And I haven't the slightest idea how they found out I am an officer in this regiment.'

His fellow-officers made it very clear they did not believe him and nothing he did was right after that. At last, he telephoned to Kitchener personally and asked for a transfer.

He was sent to a Sportsmen's Battalion as adjutant a few days later.

He slept at his house at Finchley while he held this post and he and Sybil were asleep one night after he arrived when there was a loud hammering on the front door.

Tiger opened it to find two M.I.5 men who asked him if he knew a man named Paul J. Selles.

'I did,' Tiger replied. 'But he's dead. The Germans killed him in Belgium.'

'We have a man with us in the car who calls himself Paul J. Selles,' the security man said. 'We felt sure he was a spy. But he gave us your visiting card so we thought we had better check with you before having him shot.'

Tiger was down the steps before they had finished speaking.

'Why, Paul, old chap,' he said when he saw him. 'What have they done to you? You're like a ghost. Come along in. We must get you to bed at once.'

The M.I.5. men and Tiger helped him up the steps and by degrees Tiger learnt what had happened to him. He had not been captured when he went back for Tiger's telescopic lens but a bullet had gone through his leg and the Germans had found him lying wounded in a farmhouse a few days later. The family which was sheltering him had already burnt the German greatcoat and dumped the rifle and helmet miles away so there was nothing to connect him with the Uhlans found dead in the shed. But he had been 'interrogated' with the help of frequent floggings and match sticks driven under his finger nails and some of the nails had actually been torn off in the effort to make him betray the secrets of the Belgian underground. When his comrades rescued him, he was scarcely able to walk and a doctor who saw him diagnosed pneumonia. As soon as he was well enough they had smuggled him on to a fishing boat which had put him ashore somewhere in Kent and then gone back to Belgium.

The two M.I.5 men filled in the rest of Paul's story. The local police had questioned him and, as he had no papers, notified the War Office. The rest has already been told.

Tiger felt, however, that the M.I.5 men were not entirely convinced, so he offered to make himself responsible for Paul's appearing for further questioning if necessary. When he left London, Paul stayed on at his house in Finchley. Sybil says she did not like him because he had 'cruel-looking hands'. Tiger says it was because he insisted on giving orders to the servants and to her as though he were master of the house.

Paul stayed about three months. His leg wound was not serious and he wanted to enlist but was turned down on medical grounds. After several refusals he gave it up and decided to emigrate to Australia. He died soon after the boat left Southampton.

Tiger had not been long with the Sportsmen's Battalion when he was asked to report to the Admiralty.

'I understand you know Turkey,' he was told when he got there. 'European Turkey, I mean,' his questioner added.

'Only parts of it,' Tiger explained. 'I was filming there during the Balkan Wars.'

'So I see,' the questioner remarked, turning over a sheet of paper which lay on the desk in front of him. 'Pathé Frères, wasn't it?'

'Yes,' Tiger admitted, greatly impressed. 'How did you know?'

'We do our best to keep track of people with specialized geographical knowledge,' the other said casually. 'You never know whether it might be useful.'

It was useful on this occasion because Turkey was now in the war on the side of Germany and the naval division in training at H.M.S. Crystal Palace under Colonel H. J. Levey (who is now D.S.O., O.B.E.) was destined for service in the Dardanelles. The Admiralty considered that Tiger's knowledge of Thrace could be transferred to the men with advantage, though Tiger was warned that he must on no account say where the division was going.

So Tiger left the Army and joined the Navy in the rank of Staff Scout Officer. His speciality (apart from carefully angled war reminiscences) was unarmed combat on which he wrote out a number of suggestions which were distributed to his pupils. I have read them and they closely resemble those taught to commandos as something new during World War II. They were in fact based largely on Tiger's judo and ju-jitsu contests when he was a boy.

Tiger's disappointment was intense when he was not allowed to go with the division to the Dardanelles. So, when someone suggested he should go back to the Army and become an Assistant Provost Marshal, he agreed at once.

After a short period of training he was sent to Weymouth where he found himself faced with the job of coping with some high-spirited Australians who had thrown his predecessor into the sea, breaking one of his legs and several ribs. The Australians took one look at Tiger's eyeglass and decided he was just their cup of tea. When they were paraded for him to address them, every man sported a penny in his eye. After their C.O. had had the pennies returned to their pockets, Tiger took his glass out of his eye, polished it and threw it up into the air.

It came down into its proper place without his moving an inch.

'Any man who can do that with a penny is at liberty to wear it,' he told them. 'Others will be put on a charge.'

He had won the first round. The second came the same evening when he called the Aussies together and warned them not to go on playing the fool. Then he challenged the biggest to fight him.

'How can I when you're in uniform?' the Aussie said. 'You'd have me court-martialled for mutiny.'

Tiger replied by taking off his tunic and cap.

'Now, what about it?' he inquired.

The fight lasted less than a minute after which the Aussie picked himself up for the second time and they shook hands. Tiger then told the other Aussies to gather round and explained that he had given his military police instructions to put down hooliganism. He went on:

'I like a bit of fun just as much as you do. Have as much as you like. I'll join you sometimes if you'll let me. But anyone who makes a nuisance of himself had better watch his step.'

He had no more trouble after that.

There is no doubt that Tiger enjoyed himself enormously at Weymouth. He liked the Australians and believes they liked him. He used to ride about the town on a white horse followed by two huge Great Danes. As A.P.M. he ranked as a G.S.O.2 with the appropriate pay and allowances.

He and Sybil and their rapidly growing family lived in five caravans which had been towed from London behind a traction engine. In spite of rationing they managed to entertain. Among their guests were Lord and Lady Molesworth whose presence was required three times to act as godparents. Another was Lady Malet who lived somewhere in Somerset and whose son Ned (he was nearly seven feet tall) used to arrive saying plaintively: 'I'm hungry. Mother has given away all our rations to the dear little village children.'

Besides the white horse and the Great Danes, Tiger and Sybil had a Shetland pony named Heather, a dog-cart, a groom named Beale, a maid named Mary and a cook whose name they have forgotten.

It would seem that a happy time was had by all—until peace came.

Then Tiger had to start from scratch all over again, without a penny except his war gratuity.

Tiger's five caravans left Dorset the way they came—
behind a hired traction engine which towed them, at three
miles an hour, to the Thames Valley. After several brief
sojourns, Tiger parked them outside a house called Whitton
Manor near Thorpe which is not far from Chertsey. Meanwhile he was doing what several million other demobbed men,
including his biographer, were doing—looking for a job and
not finding one. In Tiger's case, it meant selling some of his
caravans dirt cheap to pay the rent.

Then he fell ill. As he lay in bed, his leg began to bleed and
soon a bullet emerged which had first entered not his leg, but
his body, during the Bœr War.

Colonel White, a retired Army Medical Officer who attended him, sent him to recuperate at an Army Hospital which
was also a mental home mainly for officers suffering from some
form of shell shock. The mentally fit inmates were encouraged
to mix with the others in the hope that it would help them
recover their reason. There was one major who had been blown
up by a mine and who continually listened on his knees with
his ear to the ground for the sound of German sappers at work
beneath him. Another knelt down and kissed the feet of anyone
who came into the room.

The experiment was finally called off when one of the unfortunate men who thought he was Jesus Christ formed a band
of disciples and insisted on Tiger's joining it on the ground
that he was a vegetarian.

Colonel White seems to have taken a fancy to Tiger and
made him a present of £500 when he came out of hospital.
Tiger did not want to take it but Colonel White said that he
and his wife were well provided for; that they had no children
and that Tiger would be doing them a favour if he accepted
it.

He used most of the money to buy Morley House, a rambling
Tudor structure at Thorpe, near Egham. It had no electric

light or modern conveniences and both Tiger and Sybil insist that it was haunted.

Sybil told me that she often had to go upstairs in the night to comfort their daughter, Daphne, then aged about three, who had woken up crying and saying that a strange man had come and smacked her. Both Sybil and Tiger told me (without knowing the other had done so) that they had seen a man's shadow on the first landing and not been able to find him when they went up to investigate. Tiger often saw a ghostly black cat on the stairs and Sybil frequently came across a little stooping dwarf who used to stand opposite a walled-in corner of an upstairs room wringing his hands. She is convinced that, if they had pulled the wall down, they would have found the clue to his distress.

Even stranger is the story of the mandolin which was snatched out of Tiger's hand while he was playing it and which went on playing in the air with no visible hand plucking the strings or holding the instrument. Sybil and Tiger both vouch for it. And Sybil, who is now living in Dorking by herself, told me exactly the same story about the unusual behaviour of a clock that I had already heard from Tiger in Bradwell-on-Sea, Essex. The clock rose slowly from the mantelpiece to the ceiling, stayed there a few moments and then came down again, still ticking.

Tiger also saw a cup of tea rise into the air and descend again without a drop being spilt. He asks me to add that this happened at seven o'clock in the morning.

While Tiger was still living at Morley House, he noticed that Morocco had come into the news again owing to the activities of a certain Abd-el-Krim el Jatabi who had raised the tribes in the Riff Mountains of northern Morocco against the Spaniards.

Tiger was a member of the Press Club. So he went up to London, asked some questions and then called on Hugh Redwood, head of the Foreign Department of the *Daily News*, which became the *News Chronicle* and is now the *Daily Mail*.

Tiger's idea was to represent the *Daily News* as their official correspondent with the Riff Army. But this might have raised awkward questions—Abd-el-Krim was, officially, a rebel. On the other hand, news from the Riff side would be a scoop, so

Redwood told Tiger to send as many stories as he liked as a free-lance and they would be dealt with on their merits.

It sounded rather nebulous and Tiger's family now numbered six. So he made further inquiries and came to the conclusion that if he could bring back enough Moroccan leather and metalwork he would make a fortune. He felt he could do with a fortune.

This time, therefore, he went to Tangier in the dual role of journalist and merchant. Having found an intermediary who would send on his dispatches, he set about trying to get in touch with Abd-el-Krim.

Every Moor to whom he mentioned the Riff leader's name immediately changed the subject.

He had almost given up hope when he met a Moor who had been educated in England and married an English wife The Moor asked him to dinner and when Tiger told his tale of refusals, his new acquaintance said:

'Well, what do you expect? Didn't you fight against us at Casablanca?'

'Yes,' Tiger admitted. 'And I wish I hadn't. But I was also the only English correspondent there who wrote an article saying that the French were in the wrong.'

'That's true, too,' the Moor agreed. 'But what do you want to see Abd-el-Krim for?'

Tiger said that, first, he wanted to put the Riff leader's point of view before the British and American public; secondly, to do business with him.

Then he added a third.

'I hold the rank of captain in the British Army,' he explained. 'I've seen a good deal of active service. Perhaps I might be of some help. As a private person, of course.'

His host looked at his wife and asked: 'What do you think, my dear?'

'He's not the type that would let you down,' she replied. 'But it's your affair, not mine.'

Her husband laughed and said: 'Quite.' Then he turned to Tiger and went on:

'As a matter of fact, Abd-el-Krim is my cousin. But I must ask you to keep that to yourself for obvious reasons. If those

French and Spanish thieves who are trying to steal my country find out that we are relatives and that I'm helping him, they'll have me murdered—even though I am living in what's supposed to be an "international zone". They'll kill you too if they find out what you're doing.'

'Oh, I'll risk that,' Tiger told him.

'My cousin thinks we're strong enough to win now. I don't,' the Moor said. 'He judges by what he learnt about the Spaniards while he was in their officers' cadet school and afterwards as a law officer. I judge by what I know about the French. The French can't afford to let us beat the Spaniards so he'll soon have them both out for his blood. That will be the end—till the next Great War. Then, look out.'

About a week later, Tiger's new friend sent for him and said:

'All is arranged. Leave here tonight, alone. Go along the sea-shore to the Villa Harris—I expect you know it?' Tiger nodded. 'Outside the villa, you will see a man who will say to you: "I am Abdullah." You will reply: "I am Abu Hanuf" —Father of a Glass. Go with him and *sala'am aleyk*—Peace be with you. And may God prosper our enterprise.'

The Villa Harris, which a former *Times'* correspondent built for himself, is about ten miles from Tangier. It stands high, a little back from the sea, and is built of light sandstone. It was impossible for Tiger to miss it, even in total darkness.

Tiger packed his knapsack and left McLean's Hotel at about eight o'clock. He got out of the town without being challenged and seemingly without being followed. Abdullah was already at the rendezvous when he arrived—a gaunt, bearded tribesman who was even taller than Tiger. He and Tiger talked to one another in Spanish when they talked at all, which was seldom.

They travelled by night and lay hidden during the day except when Abdullah went off to buy food, mostly dates, and draw water. It was three nights before Abdullah halted and said:

'I leave you here, Abu Hanuf. Beneath the tree yonder you will find a goat tethered. Unloose the cord, take it in your hand and the goat will lead you to men who have knowledge of your coming. Go with them without fear and peace be with you.'

The goat led him to a one-storied clay house where Tiger found six armed men who led him through the mountains to where Abd-el-Krim and his men were encamped. They lived in tents which they moved each night, partly to prevent the Spaniards from taking them by surprise and partly because they themselves were constantly on the move attacking the Spanish guard-posts where they were least expected.

The country from which the Riff leader operated was mostly bare and desolate with scattered olive trees and aloes and, here and there, clumps of date palms. Sometimes, the rocky mountain side had been terraced and soil brought with infinite labour on camel and donkey back. Tiger even saw goats carrying little bags of soil on their backs. Most of it came from a valley Tiger never visited though it was only a few miles from the cave which became the centre of his activities. But the local soil had to be mixed with soil from Tangier, two hundred miles away, to give the best results. The 'fields' were seldom more than a few square yards in area and the roots generally had to be content with less than a foot of earth before reaching the hard rock. Most of the husbandry was done by bare-footed women and small children. The women wore long white dresses and went about their work veiled—at any rate when there were any men in sight.

Many of the old men who were incapable of bearing arms spent their time at little primitive forges. One group had a field forge captured from the Spaniards and when Tiger could spare the time he would watch them making gun barrels out of iron piping—also brought from Tangier. Before the barrels were fitted to their stocks, they were bound with steel and copper wire to minimize the effect of bursts. These primitive weapons were only for use in an emergency. Most of the tribesmen were armed with rifles captured (and sometimes bought) from Spanish soldiers.

When the Spaniards shelled the Riff position, Abd-el-Krim would retaliate with a home-made cannon, firing round shot like those Nelson used at Trafalgar. Tiger found this gun mounted on rails and fired from the mouth of a cave. It had to be dragged forward, but the recoil took it back again. The flash made by the explosion of the charge was so bright that the Spaniards must have known exactly where it was and one lucky shell might have put it out of action for good. Also, the fumes from the gunpowder hung about in the cave, so that it was impossible to fire the gun more than about once an hour.

Tiger suggested they should camouflage the entrance to the cave on the lines followed during World War I. Some netting was produced and set in position; then he and Abd-el-Krim clambered down the hillside to inspect the result. The Riff leader was impressed and told Tiger so.

Tiger's reply was to suggest that it would be a good idea to bring back one of the French '75s' the Spaniards were using and instal it in place of the home-made cannon. Abd-el-Krim immediately agreed.

The Riffs had captured several of these weapons before, but hitherto they had destroyed them and left them where they were. When the next one fell into their hands about a week later, the tribesmen man-handled it back to their lines and up the rocky hillside with rhythmic appeals to Allah as they heaved it over an obstacle.

'*La illaha il Allah,*' the man in charge repeated in muffled tones lest the Spaniards should hear.

'*Wa Mohammed rasoul Allah,*' the men chanted softly in unison, heaving with each invocation.

The first phrase meant: 'There is no God but God!' The second declared that 'Mohammed is the Prophet of God!' They may still be heard wherever Moslem labourers are at work from Morocco, Dahomey and Nigeria to the Philippines.

Tiger next turned his attention to the cave in which the new weapon was to take the place of the old. He saw that it would be comparatively easy to make another entrance at the side enabling air to be drawn in to drive out the fumes caused when the '75' was fired. Another advantage of a side entrance was that by laying curved rails instead of straight ones, the gun would be completely out of harm's way if a Spanish shell happened to burst inside the mouth of the cave.

Abd-el-Krim accepted both suggestions after which Tiger had to supervise the old blacksmiths while they bent the rails to a suitable curve on the field forge. It was a delicate operation. If the curve were too great, the gun might jump the rails and be smashed when the recoil drove it back after it was fired. The same might happen if the degree of curve was not exactly the same on the two sets of rails.

As Tiger watched the negro slaves blowing the bellows and the venerable smiths hammering and wrenching with their primitive equipment, he began to think they would never do it. But they did.

Tiger's success made Abd-el-Krim come to rely on him as a kind of unofficial tactical adviser and they often discussed the best way of dealing with the guard-posts the Spaniards had erected to try to keep the Riff leader from extending his hold on his country. The history books say that Abd-el-Krim had a number of European advisers and even some aeroplanes. It may be so, but Tiger says he never saw either. To the best of his knowledge the only European besides himself who visited the Riff leader was Ashmead Bartlett, the famous newspaper correspondent, who rode up one day on a horse at the risk of his life—Tiger still does not know why the Riff guards did not shoot him or how Ashmead Bartlett found out where Abd-el-Krim was.

Tiger did not even know Ashmead Bartlett had arrived until Abd-el-Krim sent to ask his advice about granting him the interview for which he had risked so much. Rightly or wrongly, Tiger said firmly: 'Don't see him.'

It was not a question of personal rivalry. Tiger himself had already sent off a number of dispatches to the *Daily News* via his middle-man in Tangier. Redwood had acknowledged the first by sending a cable asking for more. After that Tiger heard nothing. He could not understand why till he got back to Tangier and discovered that the middle-man had made off with all Tiger's money and thrown the dispatches into a corner where Tiger himself found them—out of date and useless.

But by that time, Tiger was too involved in other matters to care. He had gone to Tangier to arrange for his first consignment of Moroccan goods to be shipped to England. They arrived at Tangier on camels: string after string of grunting beasts in slow motion carrying brass trays with inlaid collapsible wooden stands, rich cushion covers, leather purses, bags—

a mass of things which the Moorish makers and traders had supplied on credit in return for the help he was giving to Abd-el-Krim.

He took the goods back to England and they sold like wild-fire. Harrods converted a whole section of their ground floor into a Moorish palace where Tiger, Sybil and the Molesworth's daughter, the Honourable Cicely, sold piece after piece while two pretty 'Moorish' girls, one of whom was really a Circassian, gave colour to the proceedings. The prices realized were fantastic. A cushion cover which had been valued in Tangier at a few shillings was priced by Harrods at sixteen guineas. Harrods took 33⅓ per cent. The balance went to Tiger, who sometimes collected as much as £4000 a week. He had displays at Harrods no less than eight times.

After London, the show moved out to the Provinces. When there was nothing more to sell, Tiger went back to Morocco to get another consignment.

During the next three years, he commuted between the two countries. He used to spend about three months in England and three in Morocco, much of it with Abd-el-Krim, whose tribesmen were the source of most of the goods he sold. He sometimes went with the Riffs on their forays against the Spaniards, feinting at one post first and then descending in force on another perhaps fifty miles away.

The Riffs never left a casualty behind. If one of their men was wounded they carried him on their backs to where they had left their horses. They tied ropes round those who were killed and dragged their bodies over the ground till they could bury them.

As time went on, Tiger found he was being shadowed when he was in Tangier. Once a man struck at him in the Souk with a dagger but his gold cigarette case saved his life. On another occasion, he saw a knife flash past him as he was walking back to McLean's Hotel. He wore a chain-mail waist-coat after that.

But it was not all so lurid. When he was strolling with a friend along the sea shore near Mogador, they came across a strange round object with a strong smell and covered in sea-weed. Tiger hacked a small piece off with a pen-knife after which the two men kicked it around like a football and then lay on their backs to enjoy the sunshine.

Soon afterwards, a ragged Arab who came up to them, pointed at the 'football' which lay beside them and said: 'Missus—you want that?' When they said 'No', he picked it up and ran off with it.

'He seems in a hurry,' Tiger's friend remarked.

They discovered why when they got back to the town. A Moorish merchant at the bar told them that the fragment was ambergris and offered £70 for it, which Tiger lost no time in accepting. Hearing how it had come into Tiger's possession, the Moor said good-bye hastily and rushed off to see if he could find the ragged Arab. He failed. He told Tiger when he got back that he had kicked between £4–500 into the ragged Arab's pocket.

Tiger was in London when he heard a street newsboy shouting: 'Riffs attack the French! Riffs attack the French! Read all abaht it!'

Tiger read and remembered what Abd-el-Krim's cousin had said. The next day, the Riffs were reported to be nearing the Moroccan capital. Soon after they were said to be in sight of it.

But they never quite reached it. Tiger says the French used mustard gas to keep them back. It is possible—the Italians certainly used it against the Ethiopians. What is certain is that Abd-el-Krim finally surrendered. The French exiled him to Réunion. He was released after World War II and Colonel Nasser offered him a home in Egypt. When I last heard of him, he was living in Cairo. It is time he was invited to go home. Morocco is independent now.

With the end of the Riff War, Tiger's trade in Moroccan goods languished. And his marriage went to pieces, for Sybil left him about the same time.

The next we hear of him, he is back in Mexico again—not fighting this time but trapping alligators and pythons for zoos and collectors in the U.S.A. and Europe.

18. SPORT, BUSINESS AND MYSTERY IN MEXICO

Tiger's first objective in Mexico was the Santiago River which rises in the mountains not far from Mexico City and flows into the Pacific near the town of San Blas where, long ago, Cortés built galleons to transport the wealth of the New World back to Spain.

Thirty years ago, the Santiago teemed with alligators and possibly still does. Tiger hired four dug-out canoes and a large, flat-bottomed boat which carried a number of long, narrow boxes with air-holes at each end and a couple of strong handles on top. Some of the boxes measured as much as twenty-five feet long—Tiger was out to capture full-grown alligators as well as baby ones.

He had a couple of rifles with him but he never used them. His 'weapons' were his bare hands and a lasso.

'Any fool can shoot an alligator from a boat,' he told me. 'But catching it alive, with your own hands, is risky. And fun. If it is big enough.'

Near its mouth, the Santiago River glides softly, smoothly, silently, through a tangled mass of mangroves. Tiger looking at them saw that their normally smooth stems were encrusted with something. What could it be? Not oysters, surely? But they looked like oysters.

They were oysters. In thousands, myriads, millions. One, about a foot above the water line, had caught a small bird by the head. Both were dead.

Each turn and twist of the river, each backwater, brought a fresh surprise. There were flocks of giant cranes, graceful and unafraid; hundreds of egrets which could have brought Tiger a queen's ransom for their plumage if he had been minded to kill them; wild duck, wild turkeys, snipe and partridges which were so tame that he could lean out of his dug-out and touch them.

The four canoes and the barge floated noiselessly on and then Tiger saw the Mexican pilot hollow his hands round his mouth. 'Honk, honk, honk,' he called. 'Grump, grump, grr-ump,' imitating the sound of an alligator calling to its mate. 'Honk, honk, honk. Grump, grump, grr-ump.' Then he signed to Tiger to go forward with his lasso to the bow of his canoe.

So there Tiger sits, lasso in hand and eyeglass in eye, waiting for his first encounter with an alligator. Presently, a long snout and a pair of eyes break surface alongside him, gently, unsuspiciously, questingly. Looking for the mate their owner heard calling to it.

Tiger's noose goes round the reptile's snout and he pulls it tight so that the alligator cannot open its mouth. Then there is a sudden swirl, almost upsetting the canoe, as the frightened creature dashes down to the bottom and then upstream. The canoe dashes upstream too, while Tiger pays out the rope as slowly as he dare. He wants to tire the alligator out but must be careful not to let it overturn the canoe.

Gradually the speed begins to slacken and the other canoes catch up. Then the alligator sinks to the mud and lies motionless. This is the signal for Tiger to jump on shore and give the rope a turn or two round a tree trunk. After which the whole party goes off to hunt for other alligators.

The next one is a comparative baby—only about eight feet long. They find it swimming unconcernedly in midstream. The Mexicans shepherd it slowly towards the bank and, as soon as the water is shallow enough, Tiger jumps out, gets his hands under the reptile's belly and turns it over on its back. One of the narrow boxes is brought and the 'baby' is unceremoniously bundled in.

When the search is resumed, one of the Mexicans spots a pair, male and female, basking on the bank of a small lagoon. They paddle on slowly, edging in towards the bank in the hope of beaching the canoes in the direct path between the two alligators and the water. Everybody is agog with excitement this time, the male alligator is fully twenty feet long and the female is not much smaller.

The canoes are quite close in before the female takes fright and makes for the stream with her jaws wide open and hissing like a steam engine. Two Mexicans lean out of their canoe and grab a leg each while Tiger drops a noose round her snout.

But meanwhile her mate is swimming straight at, and under, the canoe which overturns, toppling Tiger and the two Mexicans into the water. The female they were holding breaks loose, and breaks one of the Mexicans' leg with her tail while doing so. Then it makes off upstream. But the noose is still round its snout so the empty canoe follows her. It is a dug-out and unsinkable. In fact, it will serve as a buoy to mark the alligator's position when its assailants care to follow it.

The injured man is carried on shore and his leg attended to after which he is put on to the barge and the party goes back to deal with Tiger's first captive. On the way, they come across a shoal of baby alligators scarcely more than a few inches long. They scoop some of them up in a net, not forgetting that even baby alligators can bite. Then they proceed to haul in the grown-up one, another twenty-footer. There are seven Mexicans, and Tiger, and it takes them all their strength. But, by the time they have pulled it to the bank, it has no more fight in it and getting it into the collecting box is easy.

The female anchored to the upturned boat is treated in the same way and then the hunt begins afresh.

Tiger was something of a pioneer at this form of sport-cum-business. And no doubt alligators have grown warier and wilier since then. But he found it easy as well as exciting and his rather coffin-like collecting boxes were soon full. They and their contents were shipped to zoos all over North America and Europe. Alligators live to a ripe old age and it is quite possible that you have seen some of the ones he captured.

Back once more in San Blas, Tiger saw his collecting boxes safely away, compensated the man whose leg had been broken, and then hired a lugger with a Mexican skipper and a crew of three—he felt he was entitled to a holiday.

His objective was the Mexican island of Guadalupe which lies some three hundred miles west of Lower California right out in the Pacific. It sounds like the French island of Guadeloupe which is in the West Indies and it bears exactly the same name as half a dozen other Guadalupes scattered about Mexico and Spain. But, even in Tiger's time, it differed from all of them in being one of the few places in the world in which to find the sea elephant. Indeed, that was why Tiger went there.

But his views about sea elephants are much the same as those of other more recent observers, such as Peter Scott, so I shall say only that Tiger, even in 1927, was worried that these huge, harmless, rather helpless amphibians would soon become extinct.

What happened at Clarion Island on his way back from Guadalupe is much more intriguing. Clarion Island is one of a so-called group, though its nearest neighbour is a good hundred and fifty miles away. Clarion itself lies isolated and uninhabited some six hundred miles west of the mainland of Mexico. It has three peaks, each about a thousand feet high and is about five miles long by four broad.

Half-way between Guadalupe and Clarion Island the lugger ran into a gale and lost her foremast. The spot she chose for doing so was about a mile from a solitary rock, called Alijos, and as the wind drove the boat unmanageably towards the pounding surf, the Mexican skipper went down on his knees and told his beads.

The crew and Tiger set to work as best they could to rig a sea anchor with the help of three spars, a sail and four buckets. By the time they had done so, the Alijos Rock was scarcely a couple of cable-lengths away. Racing against time, they cut the broken foremast away, re-stepped the mizzen mast in the socket of the foremast, and managed to set a close reef sail. Having done so, they re-manned the rudder and hoped for the best which, so far as Tiger could see, was that they would not all be killed when the vessel struck: except that it might be better if they were killed. There was no vegetation or water on Alijos and the nearest inhabited land was some three hundred miles away.

Then the wind veered a few points and the lugger cleared the rock by a few feet; the sea anchor didn't. As its cable snapped, a short length whipped back into the lugger, caught the kneeling skipper on the shin and sent him scudding along the deck on his back with a sprained wrist and no skin on either leg from his ankles to his thighs.

The others picked him up and carried him below where they put him in his bunk with a bottle of rum after which they started to repair the galley which had been nearly cut in two when the foremast went overboard. As they were doing so, there was a crash and they saw that the jury mast had unshipped itself and gone over the side. They managed to get the mast on board again but the sail defeated them so they paid it out and let it serve as a substitute sea-anchor until the wind went down.

When the gale had finally blown itself out, they succeeded in hand-winching the sail in. But by this time, Tiger realized that no one on board could possibly know where they were. The lugger carried no instruments. The skipper's father had always sailed by D.R.—dead reckoning. What was good enough for the skipper's father was good enough for the skipper. When Tiger asked him how he expected to find Clarion Island, which lies about three hundred miles south of the Alijos Rock, the skipper grinned and replied that he 'knew the way'.

Tiger knew from experience that an Arab can find his way over a desert where there appear to be no landmarks. But here was a man who claimed he could do the same on the sea—a man, moreover, who had been lying in his bunk for twenty-four hours with a sprained wrist and a bottle of rum, while the sea had driven the lugger hither and yon and mostly out of control.

Nevertheless, Clarion Island duly hove in sight and they dropped anchor in Sulphur Bay as the sun went down. Fifteen minutes later and they would have had to cruise around outside till the sun rose again. It was a wonderful evening and they ate their supper on deck in the moonlight with the shore dazzlingly white ahead of them framed in the sombre peaks towering into the velvety blue night. The sea was golden with myriads of marine infusoria and animalculae. So romantic was it that Tiger pulled out his banjo and started to sing sea shanties. Soon the Mexicans joined in, though they did not know the words. They had just rollicked down to Rio, when they heard a beautiful flute-like voice from the island singing 'Shenandoah' to the accompaniment of a ukulele. From then on, and far into the night, Tiger and the girl played and sang by turns.

But who could the mysterious singer be and how had she reached the island? The skipper and crew declared that Clarion Island was certainly uninhabited, indeed, uninhabitable. The skipper swore the singer must be a siren trying to lure them to moral and physical destruction. The crew were inclined to agree with Tiger that it would be a glorious death. They spent the rest of the night, between songs, arguing about it. Finally, they drew lots to decide which of them should stay aboard the lugger with the skipper while the other three went on shore for death or glory and the girl. Tiger lost.

The sea looked like shot silk when the lucky three set off in the dinghy at dawn. A coral reef barred their way to the beach and it was some time before they could find an opening. But eventually, Tiger, watching eagerly through his binoculars, saw them beach the dinghy, scramble over the dazzling sand into a maze of cacti, black lava and huge boulders. Then they disappeared.

By daylight, the island which the moon had turned into a place of enchantment, looked forbidding and inhospitable. The sea, on the other hand, was even more magical in the sunlight than on the previous evening. Fish of every size, shape and colour darted through the wide bands of vermilion, blue and green water like rainbows and streaks of fire. One looked like a peacock with a many-hued tail that shimmered beneath the illimitable transparency of the sea. The air overhead was alive with myriads of terns which settled on the deck and on Tiger's head and shoulders. He kept one as a pet and it soon taught itself all manner of tricks.

But, as Tiger watched, a giant octopus with tentacles twenty feet long came to the surface, looking like a huge spider with a cruel beak. One of its tentacles coiled round the lugger's rail and stayed there. Another slithered forward in the direction of Tiger's face.

It revolted him and he whipped out his revolver. The shot caught the octopus between the eyes and a stream of ink squirted all over Tiger and over the surface of the sea. He went below to clean himself and when he came back on deck, he counted thirty-eight sharks. He assumed that the octopus was dead and that the sharks had been tearing it to pieces.

Just before sunset, the dinghy returned, its occupants thoroughly tired and disgusted. They said they had combed the island at every conceivable angle and found no sign of human, or other, life, least of all a *señorita simpatica*. They were all for sailing at once before the wind got up and drove them on to the coral reef.

Tiger declared that nothing on land or sea or in the air was going to stop him from looking for the lady himself. So they spent the evening as they had done the previous one, except that this time Tiger brought out his H.M.V. portable. The air was all theirs till they were about to turn in when suddenly the flute-like voice began again, as clear and distinct as crystal, singing 'Love's Sweet Song', 'Just a Song at Twilight' and other ballads. All English ones, so presumably she was not a *señorita*.

The dinghy's crew said they could not make it out. Tiger said he could: they were just a bunch of nitwits with no eyes in their heads. He was prepared to bet, he added, that he would trail her before midday. But there were no takers.

The next morning, Tiger set out alone and unarmed, except for a concertina. He scrambled the whole length and breadth of the island, climbed the three peaks in the tropical sun and, at intervals, sat down to play 'Shenandoah', 'Love's Sweet Song', and 'Just a Song at Twilight', in the hope of enticing the lady from her hiding place. But she never appeared.

The nearest approach to human beings he came across were some balloon fish with faces like little old men. He found them swimming, tadpole-fashion, in little pools of sea-water scattered among the black lava. They were only a few inches long but when he picked one up it swelled quickly to the size of a football.

When the sun began to glow like a golden football on the horizon, Tiger hurried back to the dinghy. But as he was rowing towards the gap in the coral reef, he saw two Manta Raya, or Devil Fish, disporting themselves in the channel.

Tiger says that the bigger of the two was at least forty-five feet long, including its whip-like tail, and fifteen feet across. Sometimes it 'leapt' right out of the water to a height of fifteen to twenty feet, shooting twenty yards through the air like a great kite and coming down with a thwack that sounded like the report of a gun.

One of these frolics brought the huge ray so close that it nearly swamped the dinghy, so Tiger decided he had better turn round and spend the night on the island. He went back to the beach, lit a fire, had some supper and then began to wonder about the mysterious lady. Would she come if he serenaded her with his concertina?

But she never turned up and she did not sing.

At least that is what Tiger told the crew of the lugger and what he told me. But his three rivals all took it for granted that the girl had become his without having to be dragged or enticed aboard the lugger. Tiger tried to argue that, if so, he would have brought her back with him seeing that the island was without food or water. To which the Mexicans replied that *sirenas* and *hadas*—mermaids and fairies—can do without either.

After the lapse of thirty-three years, Tiger still believes there really was a girl on the island. So, if she reads this book, I hope she will now come forward.

The lugger returned to the mainland in due course and deposited Tiger at the little port of Mazatlan from which he intended to go python-snaring in the Mexican jungle. While waiting for his guide and helpers, Tiger put up at a small *fonda* where he had a gay time dancing the tango with pretty *tanguiestas* who, between dances, insisted on sitting on his knee from which vantage point they tried to persuade him to let them see if his masonic ring would fit their slender fingers and also to let them look inside his note-case.

He escaped at last and went up to his room. Before getting into bed, he threw open the french windows and, finding the night air entrancing, pulled his bed out on to the veranda. Then he lay down, occasionally stretching out his hand to pluck grapes from the vine which covered half the railing. On the other half was a creeper with yellow, scented blossoms and its stems intertwined with orchids. A night watchman went on his rounds below, calling the hours and the weather while church bells and clocks made an almost continuous clamour. But he soon went to sleep.

At about four o'clock, something woke him, suddenly, excitingly. The moon had gone and the night was as black as lava but he could hear a soft rustling. It was not the wind.

He stretched out his hand and touched the vine stem. It was trembling. Somebody was climbing it. Somebody heavy, by the way the vine moved.

Tiger took his revolver from under the pillow, slipped very quietly from the bed, crawled on his hands and knees back into the room and lay flat on the floor against a wall. What a fool he had been to leave his window open! He had been warned a dozen times that, if he did so, a *ladrone* would come up and help himself to everything he could lay his hands on. Rich Englishmen—all Englishmen were rich then—were the natural target of every robber—and beggar—in the town.

Curiously enough, the idea of closing the window before the *ladrone* arrived, simply never occurred to him.

Presently he heard a soft thud—the intruder must have climbed over the balcony railing and misjudged the height to the floor. Then Tiger heard him creeping into the room, along the wall, the very wall Tiger had picked to lie against. So Tiger inched himself imperceptibly into the middle of the room.

Suddenly, with tropical swiftness, daylight arrived. The prowler was the Mazatlan equivalent of a house cat which in Mazatlan was not a cat at all but a snake—very like the pythons Tiger was about to start hunting but quite domesticated and friendly. This one was about sixteen feet long, quite capable of swallowing a child of, say, three, if it had been so minded. Its job was to catch rats and mice.

Some of Tiger's friends in Mazatlan also kept tame spiders to catch flies. He says they were not unlike the deadly tarantula to look at, with short, fat, hairy legs and fat hairy bodies, nearly as long as a man's little finger and nearly as broad as they were long.

The district Tiger's guide advised for his python-snaring was a long way to the south of Mazatlan, back along the caravan route between San Blas and Tepic which lies about sixty miles inland and to the east. Tiger and his party left San Blas well before sunrise to avoid being forced to ride all day behind a crawling line of pack mules. The trail—it was not yet a road—was too narrow for passing. Nor did any caravan ever dream of pulling in to the side to let a faster-moving party go by.

'After all,' Tiger explained to me. 'Why should they? They don't like dust any more than you do.'

And the dust on the Tepic Trail was of an even more noxious quality than the dust he had met behind the French Foreign Legion near Casablanca twenty years previously.

Tiger's party carried food for men, mules and horses for three weeks. They reached their chosen camping ground in the late afternoon. It was the site of some ancient city, teeming with poisonous snakes, scorpions, tarantulas, lizards, of which they hoped to secure many dozens as specimens without having to go farther afield. The pythons were there too—in the jungle which hemmed the ruins in. The ruins themselves were almost invisible beneath a tangle of orchids, creepers and undergrowth. The air was full of a scent like Californian poppies.

It was also so full of flies that you could not open your mouth without some getting in. And, when you opened a tin of jam, or condensed milk. . . .

The only remedy the Mexicans knew was to build a ring of smudge fires and sit inside it. But then the smoke not only got into your eyes but into your mouth, nose, lungs and stomach as well.

On the following morning, the flies were reinforced by flying beetles and by what Tiger describes as 'red, flying centipedes with millions of legs and horrid-looking pincers, a bite from which made you sit up with a jerk'. In the evening there came a cyclone of hot wind, heavily charged with sand which stung like a whip. And, after a night of utter discomfort, a perfectly lovely day. The flies had all gone except the millions which lay dead all over the camp till they had been swept up and burnt. And the smoke from the camp fires no longer choked but coiled lazily up into the air like plumes of egrets' feathers.

But the nights still held terrors. Before you went to bed, a fire had to be lit to drive out the scorpions from the spot on which you intended to lie. After you went to sleep, you might be woken by a giant spider, which might or might not be a tarantula, walking over your face. Once Tiger was woken by two huge Monitor lizards using his head as a highway. They were harmless, of course, but instead of going to sleep again, he brought himself back to normal with tots of lemon and rum.

The ruins and the nearby jungle were alive with parrots of all sorts, descriptions, sizes and whistles about which the only thing Tiger can say is that the birds did not whistle in unison and made more decibels of noise than he has ever heard in his life before or since. He decided to catch some to offer to his customers. It was quite easy to start with. Then a macaw nearly nipped off a finger of one of his Mexicans so he set it free in case it should do more damage. After that, not a single bird would let him come within reach. In any case, he was there to catch pythons.

Tiger assures me it was surprisingly easy. One typical day's hunt brought him no less than seventeen, the longest of which measured nearly thirty-five feet. First you find your python, then you gather round it at a respectful distance and poke at it with a forked stick, the business end of which has a piece of canvas tied to it. The python soon gets its teeth entangled in the canvas whereupon you give the stick a sharp jerk, turn the prongs over the reptile's head and press them firmly into the ground. Finally, everyone dashes forward, picks up a yard of snake and bundles it tail first into a large, porous canvas bag. When most of it is in, you can slither the rest in, especially the head, without danger of getting bitten. But it is advisable to close the mouth of the bag without wasting time.

The bags Tiger used had two 'mouths', one above the other. This enabled him to put several snakes in each bag. Each fresh capture went first into the top half. When the upper 'mouth' had been re-fastened, the lower one was opened and re-secured as soon as the newcomer had slithered to the bottom.

Tiger considers that snakes more than twelve feet long are too big to be pronged safely. The way he caught the bigger ones was to get them angry by throwing sticks at them while Tiger himself stood by with a lasso, ready to fling it as soon as the snake lifted its head from the ground to retaliate.

As soon as he had roped it, his Mexicans drove two strong stakes into the ground, each with an iron ring attached. The free end of the lasso was then passed through the rings after which the men pulled one way and the python the other.

The men looped the rope round a tree trunk and sometimes took a rest. The python went on pulling all the time. As soon as its head was safely in the rings, the men tied the rope to the tree and left the reptile to lash itself into a state of complete exhaustion while they went to look for—and lasso—another python.

Tiger's canvas bags soon became so full that he had to send to San Blas for more. Meanwhile he amused himself trying to explore the ruins which he was sure were full of hidden gold. But the undergrowth was much too much for him. The forests around were equally untapped mines of wealth: ebony, iron-wood, mahogany, dozens of different acacias stretching feathery leaves fantastically high into the air. And beneath the giants, a tangle of morning glories, bougainvillæa, orchids and scented climbing plants in bewildering variety and profusion.

There was one remarkable tree which Tiger found growing by itself in a clearing. It had no leaves, but only clusters of yellow, tulip-like blossoms on whitish branches and looking like paper flowers glued to sticks.

When Tiger had all the captives he needed, he made his way back to Mazatlan. He soon left the jungle behind and came out into a dry belt where no rain had fallen for months. The water holes were dry and the whole party, especially the horses and mules, suffered agonies from thirst.

They came at last to an isolated Indian village. The head-man welcomed them and told them to take what water they needed but to use it sparingly because there were scarcely a dozen bucketfuls left for each household and it must last them till the rains came.

It was impossible to go on until it rained, so Tiger and his party spent that night in the village. And the next night. When Tiger woke on the third morning, he found the villagers busy pouring all the water that was left into buckets which they then carried up to the roofs of the houses. As soon as this had been done, the villagers put on their festival clothing and paraded up and down the village street. At a given signal all the water was tipped on to their heads.

For a few minutes, the street was covered with tiny steaming puddles. Then the steam, and the puddles, vanished and the road was once again as dry as an oven because there was not a cloud in the sky and the village lay not far north of the equator.

That night the clouds gathered, the heavens opened and the rain descended as Tiger had seldom seen rain descend before and when he spoke to the headman about it, the man assured him that the libation had never been known to fail.

Tiger confesses that he was fascinated by Mexico. Yet he has never gone there again. On his way home via New York he happened to go to Madison Square Gardens where he saw a Hawaiian dive into a pool to wrestle with an alligator. Tiger watched enthralled as the man swam to the huge saurian which was about eighteen feet long, caught hold of its snout and wrapped his legs round its heaving body with its lashing tail. A few hectic moments followed and then, suddenly, the alligator lay helpless and quite still on its back.

'If he can do that,' Tiger said to himself, 'so can I.'

And that was how, at the age of forty-six, Tiger acquired a fresh accomplishment—wrestling with alligators in their native element.

A PICTURE of Tiger in a New York newspaper shows that in order to 'throw' an alligator all you have to do is to get one hand round the reptile's head and shoulders which, of course, is child's play provided the brute keeps its mouth shut till your hand is in position. Then you wind your legs round its body where obviously you are out of reach of its tail provided the creature is more than about fifteen feet long. And, meanwhile, you hold your breath, in every sense, because alligators naturally dive when they feel something gripping their snouts.

Unfortunately the picture does not show what Tiger's other hand is doing, which is a pity because Tiger says it holds the key to the whole business. Actually he was reaching out with it to stroke the alligator's stomach, the truth being that alligators are—ticklish.

And that (according to Tiger) is all there is to it. In a matter of moments, the alligator can be turned over on its back with its shoulders well and truly on the mat. Personally, I intend to take his word for it. I prefer tickling trout.

Tiger found alligator-tickling exciting enough but unsatisfactory as a profession. It was a one-man act in somebody else's circus. Tiger wanted a whole-time show which was all his own.

So, very soon, we find him with a little Big Top which held about six hundred people. He called himself 'Rais Sarll' and charged two shillings for admission to a show and fourpence to look round between performances. He concentrated mostly on the Thames Valley but I have found records of his having gone to Southend, Catford, Chester and other places. Many of his 'acts' involved hypnotism, especially of alligators and pythons. An article in a Berkshire newspaper describes how he dominated 'a vicious crocodile' by means of 'a sibilant whistle, a gesture of his arms and the dangling of a small brass bell'. The reptile's 'struggling legs became lifeless and the ugly head fell back'. Then a 'quick movement of the hands . . . brought back life to the reptile's limbs.'

Tiger also wound a fourteen-foot python round his neck like

a scarf. Another newspaper quotes him as saying: 'It's only a matter of tuning-in to the creature's wave-length as you would tune in a wireless set.'

Nevertheless, he had awkward moments. Once in Reading, a python which was coiled round his neck and body started to constrict. It was about twenty feet long, quite big enough to have crushed a horse before trying to swallow it. Tiger caught hold of the snake's head. A policeman who happened to be standing nearby asked politely: 'Excuse me, sir. Are you in difficulties?' When Tiger gasped 'Yes,' he seized its tail and walked round Tiger several times unwinding the coils.

Another python swallowed one of his arms nearly to the shoulder. A python's fangs are set backwards to help its dinner down and Tiger's arm is still scarred from his efforts to pull it out against the pricks.

At Chester, and I quote a local paper called *The Chronicle*, 'a villainous-looking alligator . . . turned and bit him on the wrist. Women started back horrified. Captain Sarll did not hesitate. Putting the reptile back in its cage, he immediately applied a lighted match to the wound, burning it.'

While Tiger's Big Top was at Shepperton-on-Thames, thieves broke into one of the cages and half a dozen alligators escaped. Tiger retrieved five of them, some from a sandpit and others from the Thames. But the other disappeared completely.

Tiger was intensely worried for a time—suppose the creature attacked children while they were bathing? It was quite big enough to have caused a fatal injury. Winter came with the alligator still at large and Tiger relaxed—he imagined the cold had killed it.

Five years later, however, he read in the newspapers that a 'crocodile' had been taken out of the Thames opposite Cleopatra's Needle. It was dead at last.

Once when Tiger was taking a van-load of alligators and pythons through London, he decided to go to the Press Club to meet some cronies and have a drink. So he parked his van in Salisbury Square and went to the bar. After a while, someone said:

'I would very much like to see these odd pets of yours. Why don't you bring some of them up here and show us?'

The suggestion was received with acclamation so Tiger went down to his van and returned carrying two or three pythons, one of them about fifteen feet long, and 'Maggie', the ten-foot alligator who played opposite Tiger in one of his hypnotizing 'acts'.

All went well for a while, till one of the journalists picked up a siphon of soda water and squirted it into a python's face. The snake went berserk and the bar cleared itself, long before closing time.

The python's resentment centred chiefly round the barman, George, who was wearing a white hat. It appears that white is to a python what red is to a bull and the unfortunate George, who was quite innocent, had to run for his life.

A few days later, Tiger received the following letter:

Dear Sir,

At the meeting of the General Committee today, a complaint was made that you had on a recent occasion let loose a reptile in the Bar.

While the Committee are convinced you did not mean any harm, I am instructed to inform you that strong exception was taken concerning your action.

The Committee desire me to tell you that they will not tolerate your bringing any livestock into the Club on future occasions.

Tiger was also rebuked by Bentall's, the multiple store owners, for taking a full-grown lion with him when he went to do his shopping. They said other customers were afraid to come in. Some friends of Tiger's whose name is van Hoorn and who now live at Surbiton told me that Tiger replied:

'But it's quite harmless. And supposing someone did annoy it so that it went for them: I've got my swordstick.'

The van Hoorns are also my authority for the account of Rat Town which was one of the attractions of Tiger's Big Top. The inhabitants of Rat Town were some twenty-five black and white Chinese rats each of which lived in its own 'house'. Each rat had its own name and would answer to no other. If Tiger told 'Emma' to go 'Home' and have her dinner, Emma alone went. All the rest stayed out in the 'street'. There was one rat to which he used to say: 'Come and give me a kiss.' It immediately ran to him, and up his sleeve, kissed him on the lips and ran down again.

Tiger somehow managed to find time to act in films in addition to running his Big Top. In the film *King of the Damned*, a prisoner (Noah Beery) is about to be hanged and the producer wanted to increase the dramatic effect by some unusual and poignant incident. Tiger suggested that while standing on the scaffold, the prisoner should ask if he might be allowed to say good-bye to the rat which had been his only friend during his long years in captivity.

Noah Beery liked the idea so much that he promised Tiger £200 pounds for it. The rat was brought, Tiger rehearsed its farewell kiss with the prisoner and then they asked the producer to shoot the scene with the leading lady wringing her hands and weeping at the foot of the scaffold.

The leading lady took one look at the rat and screamed. In fact she went on screaming till the rat was removed. So Tiger lost his £200. But Noah Beery gave him fifty out of his own pocket.

Besides rats and lions, Tiger had a tame gorilla which lived in his own caravan. I cannot say I was surprised when he told me it taught itself to smoke, even to the extent of lighting its own cigarettes—Tiger's example was continuously before it. But I must admit I was taken aback when he insisted that he came home one cold evening cursing himself for having forgotten to light the fire before he went out, and found that the gorilla had lit it for him.

In his opinion, young gorillas are more lovable and more intelligent than chimpanzees. But at four years of age, they begin to develop characteristics which make them unreliable— indeed dangerous—as pets.

When autumn came, Tiger used to close his Big Top, leave his menagerie in charge of an assistant and go off on his own to arrange for new shows. To a large extent, his movements are no longer traceable and he himself has forgotten most of them. But obviously he went back to Morocco sometimes because the newspaper accounts of his Big Top often refer to a 'Moorish Bazaar' in which Captain Sarll—or Rais Sarll—displayed, and sold, 'treasures from the Orient'.

He certainly used to paddle his canoe across the Channel on occasions and once he challenged a meat-eater to race him from Oxford to Calais. The meat-eater won the first 'leg' which was as far as Westminster, but then he seems to have retired, leaving Tiger to complete the course alone. Among Tiger's very miscellaneous and fragmentary archives is a letter from Admiral Mark Kerr congratulating him on having beaten 'the beefeater'. It was about this time that he paddled into a practice R.A.F. bombing area by mistake. He is quite a sizeable target but they just failed to hit him.

Another of his sidelines was salesmanship. At one time, Walls took him on temporarily when they were trying to persuade shopkeepers to use refrigerators to keep their ice-creams cold instead of 'snow' which appears to have been some sort of dry ice. They bought a hundred or so themselves expecting to be able to resell them to retailers.

Walls' own salesmen were used to selling ice-cream but not refrigerators and had no success whatsoever so Tiger, hearing about it by chance, offered to see what he could do.

His first call, in top-hat, frock-coat—full Toronto cabman's outfit, in fact—was at a shop which had firmly said no to a refrigerator.

'May I have an ice, please,' Tiger asked. 'A vanilla one.'

When it was brought to him, he smelt it, then took it to the window where he examined it through his eyeglass. Finally, he went back to the counter and said:

'I'm sorry. But I'm afraid it's no good. May I have a cup of coffee? Oh, by the way, how much is the ice? Of course I'll pay for it.'

While he was drinking his coffee, the proprietor came to apologize and to say he would not dream of letting Tiger pay for an ice he couldn't eat. Tiger thanked him, said he realized it must be difficult to prevent ice-creams from going bad and then, seeing chess-boards on a table, invited the proprietor to play. He doesn't remember who won. But he is quite sure he never mentioned the word refrigerator.

His next call was on a shop a few streets away whi

also turned refrigerators down. Tiger again asked for an ice. But, this time, when he handed it back untasted, he remarked:

'It's curious. I've just had the same experience at X's. I can't understand why you chaps don't use refrigerators. I believe they're quite cheap and, of course, there's absolutely no wastage.'

'That's true,' the proprietor agreed. 'I'll have to think about it.'

Having scattered his ground bait, Tiger left the two fish to nose at it for a couple of days. Then he went back to X and said to his chess opponent, who greeted him like an old friend:

'I've just heard that Y is considering buying a refrigerator for his ice-creams. So I dropped in to tell you. I thought you might be interested.'

'The devil he is,' X commented. 'Thank you very much indeed. Do you happen to know how much a refrigerator costs and where I can get one?'

Tiger considered the matter for a moment.

'I'm afraid I don't know,' he said at last. 'But it's possible Walls have some. I know their wholesale manager, Mr. Bennett, and if you like I'll ask him.'

X having gratefully given the 'all clear', Tiger went back to Y.

'I've just heard . . .' he began.

Y, like X, was extremely grateful and when Tiger added that his friend Mr. Bennett had told him the refrigerators were selling like hot cakes, Y picked up the phone and placed a firm order at once. Whereupon Tiger went back to X and said he had been in touch with Mr. Bennett who had just sold the last refrigerator but one to Y but had promised Tiger he would keep the survivor for X till the following morning.

He didn't have to wait that long and Tiger declares that all the refrigerators were off Walls' hands within a month.

In addition to salesmanship for others, Tiger marketed a number of products of his own. Three of these (which he called 'Wonder Working Wares') were based on formulae given him by a Jain priest whom he met—in Morocco of all places. One was a pomade to cure baldness; another a rejuvenator which was prepared from seaweeds and worked 'through the thyroid gland' and the third an eye-lash grower. Tiger's archives contain glowing testimonials for all three, including one from Admiral Mark Kerr for the hair restorer. The preparations sold well for several years but he had to stop making them when World War II started in 1939. He could no longer get the ingredients.

I am sure Tiger did not in the least mind losing the Wonder Working Wares, nor the quite considerable income they brought him. What cut him to the quick was that the war forced him to kill his beloved animals and reptiles because he could no longer feed them. He shot them himself—he could not bear to let anyone else do it.

So there was Tiger, in the autumn of his years, and of 1939, once more with nothing except a few priceless antiques which were unmarketable in wartime and which he would never sell anyway, because they are heirlooms. He was out of luck, out of a job and fifty-seven. Too old to be a soldier.

Or was he?

It was worth trying, anyway.

O F course the War Office turned him down—it always had.
But he soon found congenial work. He was a fire-fighter
for a time with the London River Police when he was billeted
at The Prospect of Whitby which he still thinks of as about the
nicest pub he has ever visited.

During most of the Blitz he was with the Auxiliary Fire
Service rushing frantically in search of the incendiaries Hitler
rained down on London, rescuing people from bombed buildings or, too often, not rescuing them because they were already
dead.

As usual, he was frequently found where he had no business
to be. He happened to be on leave when Churchill appealed
for the 'little ships' to go to Dunkirk. Tiger responded by
paddling his canoe over. He only rescued one person, a French
girl of about seventeen who implored him to take her back to
England. He compromised by putting her on board the
Daffodil, the pleasure steamer which now plies sedately between
Southend and Calais in summer. Then he went back to the
job he had set himself—salvaging ammunition and, especially,
rifles which he carried to the nearest destroyer and then went
back for more.

During one of his trips ashore, he was surprised by a party
of German soldiers, all very young lads one of whom ran his
bayonet through Tiger's arm. The German N.C.O. in charge
was older and had been a waiter in Soho. He told Tiger to
'beat it' adding: 'I wish I could come with you. I'm fed up
with this bloody war. Heil Hitler!' But the way he said the
last word but one sounded to Tiger not unlike another rather
similar four-letter word.

By the end of 1940, four of Tiger's sons and three of his
daughters were in the R.A.F. Two of his sons were awarded
the D.F.C., one of them for bombing the bridge at Maastricht.
Tiger decided that if his children could get into the R.A.F. so
could he. How he managed it, I have no idea. But, very soon,
he was a Pilot Officer and before long a Flight Lieutenant in

which rank he was expected to salute his sons, one of whom was a Wing Commander.

Flight Lieutenant Sarll was in command of the machine gunners who protected an airfield in Derbyshire against landings by enemy parachutists which, exasperatingly, never materialized. They nevertheless had to turn out every time the air raid warning went, so that a harassing time was had by all for many weary months. When Tiger was not standing by to deal with non-existent parachutists, he was teaching unarmed combat once more and also running a concert party which he called the Rafats and which raised thousands of pounds for R.A.F. charitable purposes besides giving a lot of pleasure to audiences and performers alike.

In process of time, the risk of invasion disappeared and Tiger returned to civil life, this time as security officer for Aron's, an engineering firm in Kilburn. He was standing in the road one day when he heard the familiar drone of an approaching doodlebug.

It cut out when almost overhead and dived before Tiger could take shelter. The next moment, twelve houses collapsed in ruins and Tiger found himself standing on his head—or rather, on his tin hat. His eyeglass was still in his eye and his pipe was undisturbed in his mouth.

But all that was left of a spare eyeglass in his breast pocket was a tiny spoonful of powder.

The advent of peace brought back the lean years. Tiger was nearly sixty-four and, though still strong and lusty, he had no training, or aptitude, for the kind of job available in the post-war world. To start on his own again required capital and the only capital he had, apart from his muscle and brain, was his war gratuity. He spent most of that on buying the fourteenth century house in which he now lives at Bradwell-on-Sea.

Today, at seventy-eight, he works as security officer at the new nuclear power station about a mile from where he lives. Each night, between seven and eight o'clock, he climbs into a powerful, but somewhat battered Standard and drives to the site where the huge pile has just been completed, looking like a materialistic mausoleum for a modern colossus.

When he gets home the next morning he does a few odd

jobs, watches jealously over the wildfowl of the district, perhaps mends a broken wing, or a leg, of a pet belonging to a neighbour, drops in at a pub, cures (and smokes) some of the tobacco leaves which grow profusely in his garden and then festoon his ceilings. Occasionally, in the afternoons, he takes a short nap, preferably on the hearthrug. More often, he doesn't.

What else does he do?

Well, dreams sometimes, no doubt.

What of?

Mostly of his next adventure abroad. He is longing to go to Abyssinia.